Finding Inner Peace reflects the values of humility and prayer that lead us to that true "close personal relationship" with Christ that is talked about by many but truly experienced by few. Your time will be well spent with this guide to prayer and meditation.

W. DAVID LANE, PHD, LPC, NCC, LMFT, AAMFT, CPCS, *author of* **Trauma Narrative Treatment** *and* **Strength in Our Story**, *Professor of Counseling, Department of Counseling and Human Sciences Penfield College of Mercer University*

Dr. Eddie Ensley is a true man of God. Here he introduces us to a new and amazing level of prayer—a level that invokes "the peace that passeth understanding." This book will truly bless you.

RICHARD G. ARNO, PHD, *Founder: The National Christian Counselor's Association*

In the midst of the whirlwind of modern life, Deacon Eddie Ensley finds a peaceful center to which he invites you. A joyous mix of Scripture and personal witness, this book will help you step out of your whirlwind to find calm and peace.

FATHER GEORGE MONTAGUE, SM, *Professor of Theology, St. Mary's University, San Antonio*

Drawing on the Scriptures and the Catholic tradition as well as on his own Native American heritage, Deacon Ensley provides moving true stories, practical meditations, and "calming prayers" so that we can encounter anew the Lord of past, present, and future, Jesus Christ.

VERY. REV. DOUGLAS K. CLARK, STL, VF, *censor librorum (Diocese of Savannah), translator of the* **Catechism of the Catholic Church**, *author of* **Prophets of Renewal**

In this very practical book on prayer, Deacon Eddie uncovers the many facets of abiding, inner peace and shows us pathways by which we can become more fully aware of God's presence and love.

BARBARA J. FLEISCHER, PHD, *Associate Professor Emerita of Pastoral Studies, Loyola Institute for Ministry*

Deacon Eddie Ensley leads us into a deep prayer life—the only true and ultimate source to overcome fear and anxiety.

DAN ALMETER, LPC, *Alleluia Catholic Fellowship Moderator*

Finding Inner Peace is a masterpiece of spiritual and psychological depth. I highly recommend this book. Pass it on, and the peace it brings.

JUDY ESWAY, *Board-certified Chaplain and Thanatologist,*
*author of **Real Life, Real Spirituality: A Guide to Healing and Wholeness***

Those of us struggling to find some inner tranquility in this frenetic world will find a road map to serenity within the eleven chapters of this compact book. This book could only be written by one who has found that peace, one who can guide us there.

DEACON BENEDICT LOCASTO, LCSW, *Director, Online Education and Distance Learning, Pontifical College Josephinum Diaconate Institute*

Ensley helps readers understand how prayer and surrender are essential if we want to know the peace of Christ. This is a perfect resource for peacemakers and those who seek God's healing touch for their own frustrations, anxieties, and fears.

BROTHER SILAS HENDERSON, SDS, *author of **Moving Beyond Doubt** and **Saint Aloysius Gonzaga, SJ: With an Undivided Heart***

Finding Inner Peace embraces story and prayer to show us that God comes to us in many ways to release us from fear and anxiety. Lovingly written!

ANN PINCKNEY, *Director of Faith Formation, Diocese of Savannah*

Finding Inner Peace touches the heart and calms the mind. Deacon Eddie Ensley helps us explore with compassion and understanding the root causes of the anxieties we all face. Each chapter's guided meditation offers a welcome opportunity in today's busy world to rest in the love and healing of God.

SARAH WIDENER, *Program Manager, River's Edge*

FINDING INNER PEACE

Easing Stress and Anxiety through Prayer

Deacon Eddie Ensley, PHD

TWENTY-THIRD
PUBLICATIONS
twentythirdpublications.com

DEDICATION
This book is dedicated to
my spiritual director and friend,
Fr. Douglas K. Clark, STL,
whose care, wisdom, and love
have profoundly affected my life.

❀ ❀ ❀ ❀

ACKNOWLEDGMENT
Many thanks to
Patrice Fagnant-MacArthur,
my private editor of the book,
for her wonderful suggestions
and help on the structure of the book,
copyediting, and support.

TWENTY-THIRD PUBLICATIONS
A division of Bayard
One Montauk Avenue, Suite 200
New London, CT 06320
(860) 437-3012 or (800) 321-0411
www.twentythirdpublications.com

Cover photo: ©iStockphoto.com/BlackJack3D

The stories from this book that involve people other than the author make use
of composites created by the author from his experience with real people in his
ministry. Names and details of the stories have been changed, at times composites
used, and any similarity between names and stories of individuals in this book
to individuals known to readers is purely coincidental.

ISBN: 978-1-62785-316-3
Library of Congress Control Number: 2017944488
Printed in the U.S.A.

Bayard

A Division of Bayard, Inc.

Contents

INTRODUCTION

We all yearn for a deep-seated serenity even in the midst of storms and conflicts. We generally call this "inner peace," or as St. Paul calls it, the "peace that passes all understanding" (Philippians 4:7). *Finding Inner Peace* is designed to help people today open the doorways to this peace. Christ knew this peace, lived this peace, and bestowed it on all who would follow him. His example pointed to a wisdom we can use to edge open the doors of our inmost selves to his tranquility.

If you are searching for peace, it is possible you are experiencing excessive anxiety and fear, or you or someone you care about carry worrisome burdens. Perhaps you have turned to self-help books on stress or watched TV programs for advice on worry. Some of that information is helpful, but it can only go part of the distance in helping us with our heavy loads.

True peace is found only in God. That's a given. This book offers ways to tap into that peace and helps you tackle impediments to finding that peace, such as painful memories or fear of the future. How to find peace in the midst of hardships such as suffering or when facing death is also discussed. Finally, the book suggests ways to share that peace with others once we have tasted it, becoming the compassionate peacemakers Christ tells us to be in the Beatitudes. Each chapter offers personal stories as well as a meditative prayer based in Scripture designed to help you find the inner peace you yearn for.

My Native American grandfather, Pop, used a phrase drawn from his culture, "walk in the soul." God's peace comes only when we allow him to walk in our souls. His is the only peace that erases anxiety and fear. The overwhelming witness of Scripture, and two thousand continuous years of Christian tradition—Catholic, Protestant and Orthodox—tell us that in many unexpected ways, God can astound us with his power to relieve our stress and worry. Christ promises us rest. In Matthew 11:28, he says "Come to me all you who are tired and heavy laden, and I will give you rest."

May the following chapters lead you to the one Source that can truly ease us, the magnificent and tender love of God.

HELPFUL THOUGHTS
FROM SPIRITUAL MASTERS

God's rest and God's peace are personal and up close. As St. Alphonsus De Ligouri puts it:

> As a mother delights in placing a child on her lap so as to feed and caress him, so our good God delights to treat [us] with the same tenderness, those who love without reserve and have placed all their hopes in God's goodness.

St. Bernard of Clairvaux speaks eloquently on the power of prayer:

> O good Jesus, from what great bitterness have you not freed me by your coming, time after time? When distress has made me weep, when untold sobs and groans have shaken me, have you not anointed (me)... with the ointment of your mercy and poured in the oil of gladness? How often has not prayer raised me from the brink of despair and made me feel happy in the hope of pardon? All who have had these experiences know well that the Lord Jesus is a physician indeed...

Letting God Walk in Our Souls
St. John of Kronstadt, Russian Orthodox priest, wrote: "Prayer refreshes...the soul, as outer air refreshes the body. When we pray we feel stronger and fresher, as we feel physically and spiritually stronger and fresher when we walk in the fresh air."

CHAPTER ONE

What Is True Inner Peace?

C hrist offers us peace, deep and everlasting peace. Even when the ocean rages and storms, stirring up swells the size of the tallest buildings, far below the surface, in the depths, there can remain an unbroken calm. This is the kind of inner peace Christ promises us.

Moreover, when the time came for Jesus to depart from his disciples, he used simple words to comfort their worried, bewildered hearts: "*Peace* I leave with you; my *peace* I give to you. I do not give to you as the world gives. Do not let your hearts be troubled, and do not let them be afraid"(John 14:27).

Peace does not mean the absence of conflict. At the time Christ spoke those words, everything was in disarray. Some plotted to kill him. Others spoke disgusting, mocking words to him. Everything seemed unsettled around him. Despite that, the very rhythm of his words showed he possessed a deep, abiding peace. This is the peace he wishes to impart to us if we but unlatch the gates of our souls.

This peace does not take away our struggles, nor does it immunize us from the times when everything seems to fall apart. Rather, it means that in the midst of hardships and difficulties, the Peaceful One can take our hand and walk with us through those lonesome valleys.

As you read these words, are things in your life stormy? You may be struggling with problems in your closest relationships, or fear of the future may weigh heavily on you. No matter what is troubling you, Christ can anchor you in his peace.

The Hebrew word for peace is *shalom*, usually translated peace but meaning far more than our English word *peace*; it represented the messianic times, what the New Testament meant by "new creation." It meant a time when all things would be at peace. The Hebrew conception of *shalom* is to be on the road to peace which, in the words of Old Testament scholar Walter Brueggemann, means to "live out of joyous memories and toward greater anticipations."[1]

The most common greeting in the Bible was *Shalom* or *Shalom aleichem*, "peace be with you." That phrase is still used and held in high esteem by Jewish people everywhere. It suggests the great time when God will bring his own peace to humankind. That peace will effect the reconciliation of humanity with God as well as with each other.

God had promised a Messiah who would announce the good tidings of peace. This promise was fulfilled in the person of Jesus Christ who, shortly after his Resurrection, appeared to his disciples and made the long-awaited proclamation.

That first Easter Sunday evening, the disciples cowered together behind closed doors because of fear of the Romans and the religious leaders. Jesus appeared among them and said, "Peace be with you" to calm their frightened hearts.

He punctuated those words by displaying his wounded hands and side through which that peace flowed. This greeting liberated the disciples from crippling fear and left them standing on their tiptoes with joy.

That peace continues to flow from his wounds to our wounds, allowing this deep *shalom* to heal our wounds and leave in their place an unbreakable inner peace.

In his book *In the Grip of Grace*, Bryan Chapell tells us about that kind of peace-bestowing love:

> On Sunday, August 16, 1987, Northwest Airlines flight 225 crashed just after taking off from the Detroit airport. One hundred fifty-five people were killed. One survived: a 4-year-old from Tempe, Arizona, named Cecelia. News accounts say when rescuers found Cecelia they did not believe she had been on the plane. Investigators first assumed Cecelia had been a passenger in one of the cars on the highway onto which the airliner crashed. But when the passenger register for the flight was checked, there was Cecelia's name. Cecelia survived because, as the plane was falling, Cecelia's mother, Paula Chican, unbuckled her own seat belt, got down on her knees in front of her daughter,

wrapped her arms and body around Cecelia, and
then would not let her go.[2]

Christ brings us peace just like Paula did. He protects by
being wounded and killed for us. He enfolds us in his protective embrace, which can summon peace from chaos. This love
that pierces straight through the soul can ease our anxiety
and fear.

The most important peace we can experience is the peace of
God's presence. We cannot be at peace in the very roots of our
being unless we are at peace with God. On the surface there
may be times of delight, storms of energy, but unless we allow
God to soak our inner being with his tranquility, we won't have
peace deep down.

God's peace can thrive despite the external battles. Take, for
instance, a fortified castle under siege. The besieging fighters,
who outnumber the defenders, make fierce noises, ranting out
threats. However, in the center courtyard of the castle there
is a flowing, sparkling fountain, with water fed from the high
mountains that makes its way to the courtyard through a sub-
terranean channel that no besieger can block. God's peace can
be like that.

We can be jangled by turmoil, inside or out; we can be overcome with sadness. Darkness can surround us, but the light of
Christ's peace can shine like a lamp within us.

The pledge and source of our peace is a deep fountain of
God's love, the Paschal Mystery: the life, death, and resurrection of our Lord. That fountain can pour into us a tranquility that the best minds cannot fathom. His peace is the very
ground on which our life can calmly rest if we but lean on him.

Then the changes life brings cannot pull us away from that resting or rob us of the sweetness of our kinship with God. Even death cannot break our peace or our awareness of it. As Alexander Maclaren puts it, "We shall but pass from an outer to an inner abiding place."[3]

As in the scene in the gospel where the boat carrying Jesus rocks and spins from a raging storm, we should not hide our anguish but, like the disciples, yell out to the one who can say to the inward and outward storms, "Peace. Be still."

God has blessed me with wise mentors. I have earned two graduate degrees and read hundreds of books on spirituality, both scholarly and popular. Yet, when I search my soul for words and images to describe inner peace, it is not to this wealth of wisdom I first turn, but rather to the memory of a white stucco cabin, not much more than a shack, sitting atop a bluff overlooking the swirling waters of the Chattahoochee, where my Ensley grandparents lived for decades.

Pop, my grandfather, never went to school and could neither read nor write. Granny never went to school either, but through an adult literacy program learned to read some. She would silently read the big white Bible that lay on the coffee table in front of the couch. At times she read aloud for Pop and me, parsing out each syllable slowly. Granny possessed an irrepressible wit and often left me holding my sides in laughter. Pop loved long silences and was the wisest and most peaceful man I have ever known.

Perhaps they were so special because of their Indian ancestry; Pop was half-Cherokee, and Granny also had some Native American blood. Perhaps it was because the two of them loved that book that occupied a special place on the coffee table, and the beautiful picture of Jesus knocking at the door on their living room wall. Likely, it was a combination of all three. Their cabin, for me, in the midst of a tumultuous growing up, was my refuge, my safety, and my strong fortress.

A Baptist Christian, Pop had likely never heard the word *contemplation*, the prayer of the deep silences. Yet contemplation, as I would describe his silence today, poured forth from throughout his personality. He could sit in his easy chair for an hour or two absorbed in holy stillness. Pop's time in the silences emptied him of fear, tension, and stress, while opening him to the nudges of the Spirit, making room for the peace of that white Bible on the coffee table in the inner recesses of his soul. Nor did Pop's prayer of quiet end when he got up from his chair; it followed him throughout his day.

Pop's calm set at peace those near him; his peace brought peace to me. When worry twisted my stomach, just being in his presence hushed the murmurings of my soul. Even when I was a very young boy, Pop could easily tell if something troubled me, and something often did. Pop's son, my father, was a wonderful and loving father when he was well, but unfortunately, he was often not well. My father had a mental illness that would come and go: paranoid schizophrenia. When Daddy was in the clutch of his delusions, he confused and terrified me. I didn't know how to express the turmoil it caused, but Pop always sensed when I needed to be calmed. He would say, "Let's go take a walk," and take my hand and walk with me along the bluff. At times, he would sing to me some chants in Cherokee, accompanied by the rhythms of his gourd rattle. Perhaps they were Cherokee lullabies. Their soft rhythms glided inside me, bringing me a tranquility that unruffled my emotions.

Ritual, too, was a contributor to Pop's profound peace. Each morning he would hike down to the river bank and chant songs to greet the first sunlight and honor the water. Cherokees call this ritual "going to water."

When I was five, Daddy started stringing incomprehensible phrases together while on a ladder at work. The plant nurse rushed him to the hospital so this episode could be treated; it was his first hospitalization. Mother chose to be by his bedside day and night and entrusted my care to my grandparents. That first night away from home my whole body tingled with a frightened numbness as I lay there between Granny and Pop. I remember not sleeping at all. When early morning came, after a quick breakfast of oatmeal, Pop took me walking on the bluff. He stopped and we both looked down at the water, greeting it.

Then he said, "Let's now greet grandmother sun," and he had me pray these words after him.

> Good Morning, Grandmother Sun, Good Morning,
> I stand in the middle of your sunrays,
> I stand in the middle of your sunrays,
> And by the Creator I am blessed.

That ritual grounded me, planted me solidly on this earth at a time when my life seemed to be flying apart. Pope St. John Paul II met with 10,000 Native Americans in Phoenix, Arizona, in 1987. A native medicine man and third-generation Catholic led the pope through a blessing ceremony and the pope told those present to hold on to their culture and sacred ceremonies. I wish Pop had been alive to see this.[4]

Most of us yearn for inner peace and seek it in many ways. All too often we turn to addictions, sex, money, or drugs to bring us a false sense of inner peace by numbing us. We may hold lots of baggage from both the present and past, perhaps a fractured and untrue self-image, which leads us to disparage ourselves and hold tight to a picture of ourselves as inferior. Perhaps we have a need to control others, hoping that a sense of superiority will make us feel tranquil and protected. Perhaps we hold tightly to unforgiven hurts from the past.

There seems to be a shortage of peace in our culture. Part of the reason for this comes from the frantic pace of modern life. We often stay connected 24/7. We can become addicted to our constant bombardment of cell phone rings, frequent messaging, and the screens of smart phones, computers, and tablets. We leave little room for stillness.

Most of us know what living without inner peace is like. It's living with our stomachs tied up in a knot, having a speeding heartbeat, sighing instead of breathing in rhythm. Perhaps we suffer from a hammering headache. Lack of peace tightens all of our muscles. We need to turn to God in prayer in order to find the true inner peace we so desperately seek.

⇒ TIME FOR CALMING PRAYER ⇐

A Prayer ❈ *Dear Lord, you are the fountain of peace, rich everlasting peace. In Jesus, you uttered Shalom to all creation. Help me open my heart right now to your peace. I give you my baggage, my resentments, my fears, my worries. In your midst, stress flows out of us like dishwater down a drain. You are the* *water that wells up into everlasting life, peace that settles all discord and quiets the raging wars within us. Enable us to say a strong resounding yes to your calm.*

Scripture Reflection ❊ Read the following Scripture slowly so that it sinks in. Let the words find a hiding place in your heart. If part of the passage really touches or speaks to you, slowly read that passage over again, savoring it. Let the Scripture lead you into the stillness of God.

The apostle Paul was beset by troubling anxious cares as he went about his ministry but maintained inner calm. The New Testament word for peace, *irene*, literally means wholeness, integration, and being totally alive. Paul captures the real meaning of the word in this passage:

> Let your gentleness be evident to all. The Lord is near. Do not be anxious about anything, but in everything, by prayer and petition, with thanksgiving, present your requests to God. And the peace of God, which transcends all understanding, will guard your hearts and your minds in Christ Jesus. Finally, brothers (and sisters), whatever is true, whatever is noble, whatever is right, whatever is pure, whatever is lovely, whatever is admirable, if anything is excellent or praiseworthy, think about such things. PHILIPPIANS 4:5–8

Guided Meditation ❀ Take time to relax and be still. Let your attention move over your body. Notice any physical pain or discomfort... Become aware of the emotions you are feeling... What fears are you feeling?... What guilts?... What anger?... What feelings of affection?... What are some of the thoughts you are thinking?... Don't judge or try to change what you are feeling or thinking. Just notice and acknowledge.

When you have noticed where you are right now, give yourself as you are, where you are, to God.

Pray this prayer or a similar prayer: *Here I am Lord. This is me right now. I place myself as I am in the sunlight of your calming, stilling care. I open myself to the unfathomable mystery of your peace, a peace that surpasses all understanding.*

Rest in the stillness several minutes. Pause in silence before God's quieting love.

CHAPTER TWO

The Peace of Living in the Present Moment

hen we see the beach and the ocean for the first time in years, it is so easy to stand in awe at the beauty of it, to be present to a reality that fills our senses. The scene fills us with peace and happiness. However, if the beach is our backyard, it is easy to grow accustomed to it. Walking on the beach becomes routine: the salt air and the dazzling blue of sky and water no longer startle us with the harmony of their beauty. Instead, our minds are filled with our job, finances, plans for the future, and even anger and pride. We lose the immediacy of the moment that can usher us into peace.

In short, we become numb to the beauty and happiness God's world can give us by living in our thoughts rather than in the present moment. We are always preparing to live, rather than living. Living in the present moment opens up streams of peace inside us.

Another way of approaching this is to realize that ordinary daily things hold the potential to bring us abiding peace. For years, my right knee caused me to inwardly groan with agony every time I walked. Finally, I decided to have surgery on the knee. After recovery, I found I could walk freely. For weeks I relished walking with little or no pain. Just walking filled me with peace until I once again became used to it.

Someone who gets over pneumonia delights in the wonder of just breathing. After a long walk in the sun, drinking water can be such a pleasure. After a long, dreary winter, the spring sun can snap us back to peace and joy. The reality is, if we take time to notice and live in the "right now" of things, we notice the peace-imparting happiness of just breathing, just drinking water, and just eating. As we find God in the smile of a child and relish the beauty of his footprints in woods and fields, our inner self is realigned and we taste a fathomless peace.

When I think of the peace of living in the present moment, I think of my Cherokee grandfather, Pop. His cabin, perched high on a bluff over the white running waters of the Chattahoochee River, overlooked a stunning scene of beauty. Bright green woods climbed up the bank of the river to the top of the bluff. Pop could spend many scores of minutes walking this area. Across the horizon, the wooded bluff of the Alabama side of the river glimmered in the sunlight.

Pop never shared with me the full secret of his silences, his deep peace, and his keen awareness of everything around him, but one day he gave me a glimpse. He would often take long walks along the bluff and through the woods. He slowly looked at the river and at all he saw. Once when he was watching I asked him, "What are you doing, Pop?"

He answered, "I'm looking at what is in front of me."

"Why? Why are you looking at what's in front of you?" I probed.

"Because," he said, "when you look long enough it shimmers and you see the glory."

He walked this world consciously, keenly, aware of the things just in front of him. When he looked, he truly looked, seeing unfathomable depths in each particle of reality. His prayer did not cease when he walked the bluff. His awareness took in the peace and the loveliness of all things in God's world.

As he sat in the silence in his chair, he became aware of his breath, of the texture of the chair, his heartbeat, and the Bible on the coffee table. He lived right here, in the right now.

In the New Testament, the same word, *pneuma*, is used in Greek to describe both breath and the Holy Spirit. Even the air we breathe can be a happiness and peace sent straight from the breath of God. Practicing this awareness of God's creation, both inside us and outside us, is nothing less than a doorway that the Spirit, *Pneuma*, Breath, opens for us, and the Spirit brings peace.

We can practice what I like to call awareness prayer, being totally in the present moment. Jesus' stories and the stories about him are full of the everyday stuff of life. The planting of seed, water, the washing of feet, tears—these basic elements of daily existence were as close to Jesus as his heartbeat. Out of such ordinary things he crafted his parables, and the gospel writers recounted the stories of his life using the same kind of metaphors and words.

Brother Lawrence, the simple-hearted and wise author from the seventeenth century, found the footprints of God in ordinary existence. He lived in the moment. He tells us:

> Natural objects were glorified. My spiritual vision was so clarified that I saw beauty in every material object in the universe. The woods were vocal with heavenly music....Oh, how I was changed! Everything became new. My horses and hogs and everybody became changed....When I went in the morning into the fields to work, the glory of God appeared and how every straw and head of the oats seemed, as it were, arrayed in a kind of rainbow glory, or to glow, if I may so express it, in the glory of God.[5]

When we open ourselves to God, we open ourselves to the dimension of awe and wonder, to an experience of peace beyond words. The ordinary shows its majesty. The sunshine will appear to have more splendor and we shall be able to feel the warmth of words expressed by others rather than suspect ill will hidden in them. We learn to drink in the beauty of each present moment. The trees, the stars, the hills, and the touch of another human being appear to us as symbols aching with a real peace that can never be expressed in words.

When I think of awe, when I think of living in the peace of the present moment, I think of children two to five years old.

The sense of life's mystery has not been bleached out of them. They take a leaf, hold it in their hands, and delight in it; they grab a spring flower and giggle with joy. Just watching a train go by becomes an adventure. Society educates much of the sense of awe out of us, but when we open ourselves to God's love, to prayer, awe is reborn in us.

In 2008, I was invited to speak at a gathering of Native elders from all over the hemisphere. There would be elders from Guatemala, Mexico, the Cherokee Nation Oklahoma, Canada, all over the U.S., plus two Native Hawaiians. They especially wanted me to tell about the spiritual tradition of my great-grandmother Mary Elizabeth Ensley, which was passed down to me from my father and grandfather.

This was one of the few times I would be speaking to a large audience that was not primarily Catholic. I worried that I would not have anything to say to such a diverse group. Though I am Cherokee from both sides of my family, I look Caucasian. Would my skin color be a barrier? What was handed on to me was personal, oral, and not written. I learned through gesture, song, body language, and heart to heart.

I am a sometimes compulsive researcher for my talks and books. I look to the treasures of Western spirituality, often poring over books written more than a millennium ago. I now had no book sources to turn to. Plus, I had been going through a spiritual dry spell. I was in burnout from so much traveling and writing. God didn't seem near. It was a time of financial shortfall and my inward parts were knotted, not trusting God to carry us through. I fretted and I found prayer hard.

My mind turned to my grandfather; there were so many questions I wished I had asked him. I thought back to the place where the stucco house had once stood. I desperately wanted to visit there to help jog my memory. However, that whole area had been blocked off behind a steel fence and locked gates with a "no trespassing" sign. Instead, I found a circuitous route to the River Walk that now runs along the river. I sat on a stone bench just below where my grandfather's cabin had stood.

Powerful spiritual feelings coursed through me. My ears rang with the movement of the Spirit. It was almost as though I had entered another dimension. I felt the presence of Pop, my grandfather. A song, a chant, probably a lullaby that he sang for me as a child, reverberated through my body. I opened my mouth and sang the song. I sat there for a long time just singing that chant. Peace flowed through me. My thoughts turned from fretting to taking in the present moment.

I sat on that bench a long time, paying attention to my breath and heartbeat, to the wind that blew on my body, to the sunlight that beat down on me. I watched the nearby Chattahoochee lapping the shore. For the first time in several weeks I lived in the present moment. Then I knew what I would do. I would live with awareness of those things in front of me and rather than write a scholarly discourse on Native spirituality, I would merely open my mouth and tell them stories about Pop.

At the gathering, when it came my turn to speak I did not know what I would say. I began to speak of how my grandfather always lived in the here and now and how that affected me as a little boy. I closed by singing the chant he taught me when I was young. That song conveyed wordlessly so much of God's nearness. There was hardly a dry eye in the audience. Then I added John Paul II's admonition to Native people to hold on to their sacred ceremonies.

⚊ TIME FOR CALMING PRAYER ⚊

A Prayer ❋ *Dear Lord, you entered our world in Jesus. Each moment we live can be filled with the grace of his incarnation. The here and now take on eternal significance. Lord, help us to be present to your wonders, small and great, especially your everyday wonders: our breathing in and out, our heartbeat, the very earth that bears our steps. Help us to delight in a moment of sunshine or the smell of rain on sidewalk or pavement. The touch of wind on our bodies caresses us with peace. May we see your abiding presence in each moment of our day.*

Dear Lord, you live in majesty beyond all telling. Help us to stand on tiptoes to experience each brand-new day you give us.

Scripture Reflection ❋ I have used the King James version for the following passage because it captures the mystery and awe of this mystery in poetic language, which more recent translations sometimes miss. It is not in dramatic ways that God comes to us, but in small ways, "the still small voice."

> And he said, Go forth, and stand upon the mount
> before the LORD. And, behold, the LORD passed by,
> and a great and strong wind rent the mountains,
> and brake in pieces the rocks before the LORD;
> but the LORD was not in the wind: and after the
> wind an earthquake; but the LORD was not in the
> earthquake: And after the earthquake a fire; but the
> LORD was not in the fire: and after the fire a still
> small voice.   1 KINGS 19:11–13 (KJV)

Guided Meditation ❊ You are walking on a trail in the woods. You hear the crackle of leaves beneath you as your feet carry you along the trail. You breathe in the breath of peace. You breathe out tension and anxiety. As you walk another person approaches you, catching up with you and walking with you. You see that person is Jesus. He says to you, "I am the one who walks beside you, always. I give you this present moment. Live, instead of practicing living. Notice the things around you, because in them you will see this present moment. Let preoccupation with the past flow out of you with your breath. Let anticipation and concern for the future slip away from your breath. Live in the eternal now where I live and you will be filled to the brim with my peace, my shalom."

Jesus puts his arm around your shoulder and you feel fear, tension, and anxiety pass out of you into him, where it disappears in the living flame of love that is his heart.

Imagine Jesus seated next to you. He calmly holds your hand, easing you into a deep peace. As you are warmed by his presence, name to him some of the ways you need him to be your refuge.

Rest a while in the stillness.

CHAPTER THREE

The Peace
of Gratitude

He who brings thanksgiving as his sacrifice honors
me; to him who orders his way aright I will show the
salvation of God! PSALM 50:23

Fear, anxiety, and anger, even in small amounts, can
weigh heavily on our souls, pushing out the inner peace
we so desperately desire. One surefire way to restore
that peace is to focus on the many people and things in our
lives we have to be grateful for.

Thirty years ago, while I was visiting a monastery in the
Midwest, I met a thirty-year-old man who lived there as a lay

associate. One evening I joined him while he was preparing some newly felled logs for an addition to the monastery. In a most unself-conscious way, he hummed happily as he worked. Then, almost as if I were not there, he began to pray softly as he trimmed a piece of a log, "I thank you, Lord, for such a fine piece of wood. I thank you, Lord, that it didn't rain and we had such a gorgeous sunlit day. I thank you, Lord, that I have a place to lay my head and companions that help me along the way."

Prayers of thanks poured out of him; as he prayed, a brightness shone from his eyes. In the eyes of the world, it seemed as though he had little to be thankful for. Alcoholism had destroyed his marriage. Although he was now in recovery, he had lost custody of his two little girls. The courts did not even allow him to visit them. He feared that a normal work environment would cause him to resume drinking, so he found surroundings much more conducive to sobriety—a monastery, where he worked for only room and board.

There was so much in his life that could have caused him stress: not being able to see his children, and not having what the world counts as regular employment. Despite this, his main mood was one of thankfulness and joy. Thankfulness chased away the distress and worry and brought peace. It can do the same for us too.

My grandparents, Pop and Granny, had hearts brimming with gratitude. Every time I entered their little house they greeted me warmly and let me know how thankful they were for me and that my presence was priceless to them. That thankful appreciation was a safe harbor from the tumult in my own home.

Granny and Pop thanked God too. Sometimes when Granny read the Bible to Pop and me, she would speak out all the things we had to be grateful for.

Pop and Granny had a favorite song, "Precious Memories." When it came over the country radio station, they listened intently. I remember the song coming on the air one day as Granny was sweeping. She stopped her sweeping, leaned on her broom, and let the words flow through her. Tears began to trace down her face. Pop's eyes also moistened.

This verse I remember from the song, even after all these years:

> Precious memories how they linger,
> How they ever flood my soul.
> In the stillness of the midnight,
> Precious sacred scenes unfold.[6]

This song sums up the meaning of gratitude. Warm gratitude and a cold heart are incompatible. Gratitude is the memory of the heart; thankfulness is the tune of angels.

I know in my own life, during stressful times, I have turned to scenes in my memory when God was near or I felt the love of others. Calm followed those memories.

Gratitude is a form of remembering prayer in which we remember the blessings and joyful times when God was near; when the world was bright and alive for us. The great Scripture passage for remembering prayer is found in the first chapter of Luke where it says: "Mary remembered all these things and pondered them in her heart" (Luke 2:19). Sacred memories and gratitude calm, heal, and bring peace to us.

Thanksgiving can also be deepened by remembering and thanking the people in our lives who have been the touch of God to us. One time when my mother was in her eighties and frail, I wrote out a letter enumerating many of the ways she had loved me. We had had our hard times, but I always knew my parents truly loved me. I gave the letter to her and she treasured it the rest of her life, showing it to nearly everyone that came by to see her. Giving that letter to her calmed and stilled our souls, bringing a special and lasting peace, not only to her but to me.

I had told my mother many times that I loved her, but the act of putting it on paper helped make it concrete. Sometimes we wait until it is too late to say thank you.

Someone else whose restless spirit was profoundly calmed by remembering and appreciating the people who had touched his life was William Stidger, a wealthy businessman who had broken apart emotionally. Conflicted and a stranger to peace, he lost his zest for life. Energy drained from him, leaving him weak and emotionally depleted. He had sunk deep into depression. Even seeking help did not provide any comfort.

Then one day an insightful friend asked William, "When was the last time you singled out one of your acquaintances who has been gracious to you and expressed appreciation?"

At first this annoyed William, but he went home and thought about it. In the privacy of his home he remembered a high school teacher who had taken an interest in him and engendered in him a love of poetry and literature. He hadn't thought of her in decades, but she was the first person who came to mind. He penned a letter of thanks to her.

In the trembling handwriting of a long-retired teacher, a letter came back to him in three days saying, "My eyes are blinded with tears as I write. You are the first student in all my career who has ever written me a letter to express thanks." She continued, "I will keep it as long as I live."[7]

After her response, he thought of someone else who had touched him, then others, and others after that. He wrote them too. His bosom glowed with peace. He didn't even notice when his depression lifted and his inner warfare ceased; such was the power of gratitude. Gratitude can calm our anxiety and fear as well.

Lack of gratitude destroys the soul. In today's society, it is so easy to believe that everything we have accomplished has been by our own will, our own self-confidence, our mastery of life.

I remember an old *Dennis the Menace* cartoon I read decades ago. It was Christmas afternoon and Dennis was seated under the tree with open boxes and wrap and seemingly countless toys up to his neck. Then he laments, "Is this all? Is this all I got this year?"

If we see our world like Dennis saw his that Christmas, we will have barren souls, be in conflict with ourselves and with others, and be strangers to inner peace.

Everything Is a Gift from His Hands

If you are feeling stressed, get pen and paper out and begin a prayer of thanks. Start with the phrase, "I thank you, Lord, for..." Next write out, item by item, all the people and things for which you are thankful. Then, unhurriedly and prayerfully, read what you have written. If a phrase strikes you, or "takes on anointing," just repeat it over and over again and let that carry you into the stillness.

As we enter wholeheartedly into this exercise each day, it begins to form a habit of gratitude that will cause a change in our lives that Walter Brueggemann calls a shift from "disorientation to a new orientation." In this new orientation, we are astounded by the love of God, by the intervention of God, and by the surprising touch of God's comfort on our hearts. Such a movement "includes a rush of positive responses, including delight, amazement, wonder, awe, gratitude, and thanksgiving."[8]

As we learn to appreciate life, we discover that blessings surround us even in the bleakest of times. Giving thanks relieves our worry and stress by turning our thoughts from just ourselves to God's goodness. Think of the last week in your life. What acts of kindness were done for you?

Focus on a person that you know loves you, someone with whom you have a current good relationship. See the beauty of that person in your mind's eye. Be thankful to God that you have someone like that in your life. Think of some of the ways God has touched you lately, and give thanks.

⇒ TIME FOR CALMING PRAYER ⇐

A Prayer ❀ *Thank you, Lord, for the beauty of this earth. Thank you for the cosmos and the immensity of its splendor and light. Most of all, thank you for sending your Son. Through him, through his dying and rising, you are remaking all creation. And I thank you, Lord, that you are also remaking me. You heal me, comfort me, console me, point me, and bring peace to my heart.*

Scripture Reflection ❊
Let your gentleness be known to everyone. The Lord is near.
Do not worry about anything, but in everything by prayer
and supplication with thanksgiving let your requests be made
known to God. And the peace of God, which surpasses all
understanding, will guard your hearts and your minds in
Christ Jesus. Finally, beloved, whatever is true, whatever is
honorable, whatever is just, whatever is pure, whatever is
pleasing, whatever is commendable, if there is any excellence
and if there is anything worthy of praise, think about these
things. Keep on doing the things that you have learned and
received and heard and seen in me, and the God of peace will
be with you.   PHILIPPIANS 4:5–9

Guided Meditation ❊   In your imagination, go to your
mailbox. There, you find a letter from Jesus. With trembling
hands, you read the letter right there at the box. In the letter,
Jesus tells you three things he delights in about you and
thanks you for choosing to be his disciple. What are those
three things?

You walk back to the door of your house and then see Jesus
standing in the doorway. Perhaps you feel unworthy of his
thanks and affirmation. Tell him about it as he listens to you.
When you finish, he says, "Be at peace, My grace is sufficient
for you. When you are weak, then you are strong."

Jesus leads you into your house and then into your living
room. You both sit together on the couch. Your heart brims
over with thankfulness. You, in your own words, thank Jesus
for all the ways he has loved you. You and Jesus embrace as
the peace of the Father flows over you.

CHAPTER FOUR

The Peace of a Pure Conscience

I met Kerry, a middle-aged man, at a retreat I led in the Northeast. He told me a story that began twelve years earlier. He woke up one morning, his head throbbing with the fiercest headache he had ever had and an ocean full of dread sitting on top of him. Kerry was on the wrong side of the padded locked room, known as the "sober up" room he had used as a sheriff's deputy to hide away drugged or drunk prisoners while they struggled toward sobriety.

Dizzy and still not fully aware, scenes from the previous day at sunset filled his mind. He had been drunk, waving a shotgun at his brother Bill in his parents' front lawn. He was filled with rage. His brother had failed to pay him for the cost of a muffler he had used to fix Bill's car and he wasn't going to stand for it. As he swirled the shotgun, it went off, killing his brother instantly. On the lawn, watching, were their parents and Bill's six-year-old son, Kenneth. His last memory of the night was being shackled and driven away by fellow sheriff's deputies to the county lockup.

As the days went on, the fathomless dread weighed down on him even more. He had killed his brother, whom he so loved, in front of the people Kerry loved most. Guilt, self-loathing, and despair were his daily meal.

He had funds for an attorney and got the best in the county, but as the weeks passed his parents did not visit, take his phone calls, or answer his letters. He was alone, utterly alone. In a plea deal, he took a ten-year sentence for manslaughter.

He was profoundly depressed; his doctor put him on anti-depressants. He improved some, but no pill could take away the guilt that weighed him down.

He was bored as the months passed by and he started attending the Catholic ministry gathering every Sunday night at the prison. Raised Protestant, he attended the Catholic gathering rather than the Protestant one because it had real time for talking and sharing with others rather than consisting primarily of the loud praise songs that dominated the Protestant worship.

Then, during one ministry gathering, the pastor of a nearby parish led Mass and confessions. Protestant attendees went to confession too. While they could not receive absolution, it gave them a beautiful chance to get things off their chests.

When Kerry went to confession, he choked up as he told the priest the story of killing his own brother. The priest let him sob for a while, then read the parable of the prodigal son from Luke (15:11–32). Kerry told me this phrase went straight to his heart: "So he set off and went to his father. But while he was still far off, his father saw him and was filled with compassion; he ran and put his arms around him and kissed him."

Kerry thought, *in spite of the prodigal's rags and the stench of the sty, the Father's love was round about him; it is round about me too.*

Then the priest asked him to imagine Jesus reaching out to him in a loving, accepting embrace. He then invited him to read and meditate on the passage about the prodigal son. In Jesus' embrace, Kerry's burden of guilt lessened. He was moved in the depths of his being; a few months later, he became Catholic.

He copied down this Scripture from Luke, mailed it to his own father, and told of his experience of confession and the astonishing forgiveness of God.

Soon a card came back with the scribbled words, "We love you and want to be in your life. Please forgive our silence." His parents visited him in prison the remaining years of his imprisonment, then opened up their home to him when he was released. When his parents met him at the bus station, they surrounded him in an embrace as heartfelt as the one in Luke. More was to come. When they arrived at his parents' home, he was greeted by Kenneth, his brother's son, now sixteen and living with his grandparents. After a moment of hesitation, Kenneth embraced him too.

God's kiss of forgiveness coming through prayer and through Kerry's family helped suck the poison from his wounds. God's forgiveness is the only scalpel that can remove our emotional scars.

When God forgives our sins in the sacrament of reconciliation or through an act of sorrow for sins, he takes them into the flame of love that is his heart where they disappear forever.

God's forgiveness does for the human heart what sunshine does for a plant: it warms it and causes it to grow. Our hearts grow large, like giants' hearts, and it becomes so much easier to forgive others.

A pure conscience means, above all else, going to this gracious God for forgiveness. That's why we say we celebrate the sacrament of reconciliation. It means a clean slate, a fresh start, and a new beginning. Absolution is a joy, not a dread.

Conscience is our moral sense of right and wrong. The seventeenth-century philosopher Immanuel Kant had the following words inscribed on his tomb: "There are two things which fill me with awe, the starry heavens above us and the moral law within us."[9] Conscience emerges from our inner sanctuary, our most sacred core.

The *Catechism of the Catholic Church* states, "Deep within his conscience man discovers a law which he has not laid upon himself but which he must obey. Its voice, ever calling him to love and to do what is good and to avoid evil, sounds in his heart at the right moment....For man has in his heart a law inscribed by God" (1776).

St. Augustine wrote: "God does not impose impossible things, but by giving his command, he admonishes you to do what you can and to pray for what you cannot do (yet)."[10]

Christian conscience is much more than memorizing abstract rules as you would in a mechanical engineering case. Instead, it is an intent to grasp God's present will for our lives, our families, our church, and this earth we live on. It means listening to the still small voice of the Spirit in all we do. It means distinguishing selfless and self-effacing love of neighbor from raw selfishness. St. Paul expresses a fundamental attitude of the Christian conscience in his Epistle to the Ephesians: "Use the present opportunity to the fullest" (5:16).

This type of knowledge can only come from our depths, and only if we are truly people of prayer constantly asking for God's guidance. "Watch therefore and pray," the gospel tells us (Luke 21:36).

A true formation of conscience involves coming to the Father often for his forgiving embrace, as Kerry did. Having an active prayer life and a pure conscience are forever wed together. Our attitude should be like Paul's: "I have not yet reached perfection, but I press on, hoping to take hold of that for which Christ took hold of me" (Philippians 3:12).

Making daily acts of contrition and sorrow when we feel we have failed God or others is a key element in having a pure conscience. In his diary, Pope St. John XXIII wrote about this when he said that if after failing God in any way he made a quick act of sorrow, he could proceed with his day joyfully, "as if Jesus had given him a kiss." Experiencing the depths of God's forgiveness in our inner core heals our emotional hurts and plants in our hearts love of neighbor and creation.[11]

A key part of developing a pure conscience must be directed toward love and forgiveness of enemies. When we forgive, we are most truly God's and most truly ourselves. In Matthew, Jesus tells us, "If you only love those who are your friends, what reward can you expect…be all goodness just as your Heavenly Father is all good" (5:46–48).

As Shakespeare reminds us in *The Merchant of Venice*, "The quality of mercy…is twice blessed. It blesseth him that gives and him that takes….It is an attribute to God himself, and earthly power doth then show likest God's, when mercy seasons justice."[12]

We also need to inform our conscience because humans can be so subjective. We need to be guided by Scripture, especially the Ten Commandments; the gospels, especially the Beatitudes; and the teaching of the church.

Pope Francis has beautifully summed up the meaning of conscience in these words:

> So we also [like Jesus] must learn to listen more to our conscience. Be careful, however: this does not mean we ought to follow our ego, do whatever interests us, whatever suits us, whatever pleases us. That is not conscience. Conscience is the interior space in which we can listen to and hear the truth, the good, the voice of God. It is the inner place of our relationship with Him, who speaks to our heart and helps us to discern, to understand the path we ought to take, and once the decision is made, to move forward, to remain faithful.[13]

There is a moving story I read in *The Little Flowers of St. Francis* that I will paraphrase for you. Francis, just a little guy, was walking along a dusty road with his close friend and confidant, Masseo, when out of the blue Masseo said to Francis, "Francis, why you? Why is the whole world following after you? Let's face it, Francis, you are not handsome: you are nothing much to look at. You are not an eloquent speaker. You are not educated: you know only a few lines of Latin. Why, Francis, is the whole world following after you?"

Francis paused a moment and then answered: "The Most High looked down from heaven and couldn't find anyone more foolish, more going his own way, and he had mercy on me. That is so that what I do could be seen as coming from the Most High and not from me."

That is the part of a pure conscience, knowing that whatever good we do is not just from ourselves but from God's grace.

As Pope Francis has told us, the church is not the gathering of the pure ones but a "hospital for sinners." God picks those who need forgiveness. Even the Apostles were a flawed and motley crew.

In the second century of Christianity, a renowned philosopher, Celsus, said something that goes to the heart of the matter when, in a polemic against Christians, he wrote: ""All other religions invite those who have clean hands and a clear conscience. But whom do these Christians invite? Everyone who is sinful, weak, and wretched, as if they were assembling a gang of thieves!"[14]

It is out of this "gang" that the saints come, and God invites all of us to be among them.

⟹ TIME FOR CALMING PRAYER ⟸

A Prayer ❧ *Dear Lord, you welcome sinners into your embrace and celebrate their coming home. At the foot of the cross you said, "Father forgive them, for they don't know what they are doing." Grant us true sorrow for the selfish way we can use you or others. We need your forgiveness each day, every day. Your forgiveness does for our soul what sunshine does for a plant.*

O Lord, you are a lavish forgiver. You forgive like a parent who kisses the transgression into everlasting forgetfulness. In the sacrament of reconciliation you toss our sins into the deepest part of the deep ocean and then put up a sign saying, "No fishing allowed." Teach us to rejoice that you hold us so closely.

Scripture Reflection ❋

If we say that we have fellowship with him while we are walking in darkness, we lie and do not do what is true; but if we walk in the light as he himself is in the light, we have fellowship with one another, and the blood of Jesus his Son cleanses us from all sin. If we say that we have no sin, we deceive ourselves, and the truth is not in us. If we confess our sins, he who is faithful and just will forgive us our sins and cleanse us from all unrighteousness.

1 JOHN 1:6–9

Guided Meditation ❋

Sit quietly; let the warm, relaxing stillness of God calm the muscles of your face. The healing warmth of God's love flows into your neck, healing and relaxing. The healing warmth now passes into your shoulders, your arms, your hands, and your back. Your stomach is quieted by the nearness of God's love.

Gently repeat "Jesus, Lord Jesus" over and over again to carry you deeper, still deeper, into the relaxing peace of God's love.

Gently, let some scenes when others have forgiven you come to mind. Feel the warmth and peace of their forgiveness.

CHAPTER FIVE

The Peace of Acceptance

A Jewish parable tells the story of a king who had a beautiful and pure diamond. An accident damaged the diamond, leaving a big scratch. In desperation, the king called for the help of the best diamond cutters in the realm to restore the diamond. They all said it was not possible; the diamond was scratched up beyond repair. Then a lapidary, a pauper at the bottom end of the social ladder, came forward and said he thought he could fix it. A few weeks later he gave the restored diamond back to the king, and it was even more resplendent than before. The lapidary had carved an exquisite rose on the diamond, using the scratch as the stem.

Some impediments, hurts, and losses won't go away, but

if we handle them right, accept them, and give them to God, God can make that which is damaged and wounded even more beautiful than before. If we give over our hurts and losses to God, accepting what we can't now change, he can rearrange them and transform them into something wondrous, just as the pauper did to the diamond.

Letting go isn't a fine walk in a meadow for most of us; it's difficult. We yearn to hold on, maintain control, and try to maneuver reality to suit us. Attempting to hold the "reins on our world" is simply tiring and futile. Clutching so tightly creates inner warfare and discord to which only the love of God can bring peace. As author Terri Fracci puts it, "There are so many things in our lives that we have little or no control over; and yet we push and bully and strive to attain control all the same."[15]

The phrase "Let go and let God" is more than a pretty slogan; it is the turnstile to inner peace. We surrender and put power where it belongs—in God's hands. When we do this, the menacing waves of anxious energy can, in time, settle down to a great ocean of calm.

We all experience losses, both small and large. Although accepting loss can be agonizing, we travel through loss and acceptance our entire lives. Every morning we experience the loss of the day before and accept an unknown new day. When we were very little, just beginning to walk, we walked with our small hand held by the larger hand of the adult. Then we let go of the safety of walking hand in hand in order to walk on our own. When we take a child to the first day of kindergarten, we let go. The same goes for middle school, high school, college, and even graduate school. When we marry, we let go of singleness for committed companionship. Letting go and accepting new realities is a constant for most of us.

Sometimes, we have to let go of our dreams: placing first in the Boston Marathon, climbing Mt. Everest, obtaining the funds and time to pursue graduate school, hoping that the person who thoroughly pulled out of our relationship will have a change of heart and come back.

Then there are huge losses, such as the death of someone dear to us, the loss of love or friendship, the loss of health, or financial setbacks. Usually when we have a big loss, we face a whirlwind of emotion. Accepting those emotions and working through them can become a springboard to healing and the coming of new possibilities and new hope.

According to columnist LaTonya Dunn, "Acceptance is not about giving up, but about acknowledging that which you cannot change. Acceptance is not letting go of hope. It is about allowing your faith to go where you cannot. Acceptance is not choosing to be unhappy, instead, it is choosing to live through the unhappy moments. They won't last always."[16]

Acceptance of impediments and limits is something that has been necessary in my own life. I mentioned earlier that I had to deal with my father's mental illness and his often scary behavior. Unfortunately, I also had to deal with something even more difficult than having a dysfunctional father, something that afflicted my soul. This was a physical disability—in layman's terms, a brain injury. I was born a footling breech and experienced strangulation from the cord wrapping around my neck three times. The doctor had to use heavy forceps and said if it had taken even a few more seconds I would have been born dead. My parents rejoiced that I was born alive. However, I was born with a hidden disability, one that was not obvious from looking at me, but was a major impediment none the less. The right hemisphere of my brain had many dysfunctions. Visual-spatial tasks such as dressing, keeping anything in order, and managing the tasks of daily living were confusing and, in some instances, nearly impossible. Adding to the damage was a concussion I suffered when I was three from running headfirst into a stone wall.

The left hemisphere of my brain, the part of the brain that controls the use of words and understanding of ideas as well as articulation, worked beautifully. My parents, even though my disability had not yet been diagnosed, surrounded me with books and read to me. I am so grateful to them for helping to develop my verbal side. But as I grew older, my deficits really stood out. I couldn't dress and get ready in the morning without help from my parents, even into my early teen years. Because I was so ashamed of my problems, some days at school I wouldn't smile or look others in the eye.

I also had some learning disabilities. I am what they would call today, "bright but learning disabled." Though my parents stimulated my verbal abilities, they ridiculed me over my visual-spatial disabilities. They just thought I was lazy. I remember one horrific scene when I was in junior high when my parents got into a shouting match over which parent had "ruined" me.

School was no better. These were the days before teachers were trained to accommodate and deal with students' cognitive deficits and learning disabilities. In junior high, one teacher told me, "You are no good at all. You never will be any good." Because I was different, some of my peers bullied me, doing things such as pushing a load of books I was carrying onto the floor, leaving me to bend down and pick them up as other students giggled.

A million tons of despair weighed down on me. I tried with all my might to overcome my deficits, but it was like punching a shadow. Nothing seemed to change. Daddy's illness had returned and it was terrifying to be around him. At thirteen, I felt life was over. I had nothing to look forward to but shame, rejection, helplessness, and possibly early death at my Dad's hands. I was also grieving for Pop, who had died a couple of months earlier.

After returning home from junior high one afternoon, I saw no reason to go on any further. The thought of ending it all passed through me. In the pit of my despair, I put a symphony on the hi-fi in hopes that music could help me forget, at least for a few moments, my hopeless situation. The symphony strengthened me, and I finally had the energy to do something I had not done in a long time: pray.

All I could mutter out was, "God, help me." I prayed those words over and over as the melody of the symphony swept over me. The room changed. A loving presence like infinite pure light filled the room and filled my soul. Even the cells of my body tingled with love made manifest.

"Who are you?" I asked. Then I heard the answer as the light spoke, without words, but clearer than words, heart to heart, soul to soul. [I will attempt to give words to a communication greater than words.]

The light answered me, "I am the one who comforts little boys who have no one to turn to."

"I am not a little boy," I responded. "I am a teenager now, thirteen."

"No, you are a little boy," the light continued, "and an inno-cent and pure one."

"I don't feel innocent and pure. I am a failure, lazy, ruined."

"Take my hand," the light told me. I reached out and a hand surrounded my hand, and I held the one who, in the midst of light, looked like I imagined Jesus looked. I could feel in that hand the scar a nail had left.

"I know someone who has never thought of you as fumbling and lazy."

"Who?" I asked.

"Think of someone who has never called you anything but good, even priceless."

"Pop," I mumbled out.

And the light answered, "Pop."

With those words, I felt all the shame, hopelessness, and despair flow from me into the nail-scarred hand, from there to the living flame of love that was his heart.

The record finished playing and the light had slipped away as surely as it had come in. I felt refreshed, hopeful, emptied out. At least for a moment, I had "let go and let God."

There were many times of despair, even after this. God usu-ally does not come to me so vividly. I have my dry times, my desert, my dark nights of the soul. But hope had found a place within me and would never fully let me go.

⇒ TIME FOR CALMING PRAYER ⇐

A Prayer ✵ *Dear Lord, you accepted the path the Father set out for you, even torture and death. You accepted each new* *day, letting go of the previous day. You knew loss, hunger, and thirst. Your heart gladdened in friendship, just as our hearts do. You suffered when friends fell away. You faced changing circumstances, accepting all that came your way. You were content with little. Through this your heart poured out love on humankind and all creation. You loved when the going was difficult. You surrendered all things into the Father's hand.*

We live in an imperfect world: a dear friend breaks our relationship and will not return calls, a beloved child becomes addicted to alcohol and drugs and nothing seems to work or help. Life opens up fresh and even wonderful new directions, but we fear letting go of the familiar, even for a happy, better future. We can be so stuck in the familiar that we cannot accept the future that is opening up for us.

Dear Lord, help us to accept life as it comes to us, turning the hard stuff of life into your hands, surrendering all things to you as you surrendered all things to the Father.

Help us to live contentedly and to accept our lot in life when change seems impossible. Help us to accept that your grace is sufficient for this day and every day. Your enormous and tender love can help us accept the things we need to accept. You are the calmer of heart and soul; calm us as we accept those things that must be accepted.

Scripture Reflection ❊

What then are we to say about these things? If God is for us, who is against us? He who did not withhold his own Son, but gave him up for all of us, will he not with him also give us everything else? Who will bring any charge against

God's elect? It is God who justifies. Who is to condemn? It
is Christ Jesus, who died, yes, who was raised, who is at the
right hand of God, who indeed intercedes for us. Who will
separate us from the love of Christ? Will hardship, or distress,
or persecution, or famine, or nakedness, or peril, or sword?
No, in all these things we are more than conquerors through
him who loved us. For I am convinced that neither death, nor
life, nor angels, nor rulers, nor things present, nor things to
come, nor powers, nor height, nor depth, nor anything else in
all creation, will be able to separate us from the love of God in
Christ Jesus our Lord.   ROMANS 8:31–39

Guided Meditation ❋ Sit still in a chair. Notice how the
chair bears your weight. In the same way, God bears the
weight of all our difficulties. Pure love cascades over you like a
waterfall, refreshing you, stilling you, quieting you so that your
heart quietly beats with God's heart and your breath comes
and goes like his breath. Fear, anxiety, and tension flow from
you. Worry ceases. Your muscles relax and you are set at ease.

Someone comes up behind you, gently taking hold of
your shoulders, lovingly massaging them with his fingers.
Instinctively, you know it is Jesus. One by one you tell him
of the things in your life that you must let go of and accept.
You feel your frustrations with your circumstances in life flow
through his hands into his chest, where they disappear in the
living flame of love that is his heart.

CHAPTER SIX

Making Peace with the Past

When we were infants and toddlers we easily screamed out our discomfort or hurt. Babies, it seems, have been gifted with especially loud lungs. If we were hungry or wet, we cried out and often got a quick response. As we grew older, we found those emotions didn't necessarily get us what we wanted and learned that staying quiet got us more approval. Thus, early on, we began the process of repressing hurt. When bad things happened, we learned to hide them way down inside ourselves.

We slowly unlearned how to let out powerful feelings and often built a wall of niceness around our hurt. There the hurts remained, like the proverbial stones at the bottom of the stream that alter the course of all the passing water.

One reason our subconscious learns to repress feelings is to protect us from the overwhelming trauma that can come from being verbally or physically abused or having to face the pain of huge losses, such as the death of a parent or sibling.

This subconscious pain may show itself as anxiety when similar things happen in our adult life. For instance, if a beloved mother died when we were little, watching a happy child with her mother can trigger a paralyzing anxiety in us.

As we go through life, a time can come when the subconscious no longer can hold it all in. Seemingly out of nowhere we are flooded with uncontrollable negative feelings and anxieties. For a while it seems like we are as vulnerable and fragile as an ignored infant.

We also experience great and wonderful things. Most of our lives also have good memories. In a sense, our lives are like the Rosary. We not only have our sorrowful mysteries, but we also have our joyful mysteries. Both joyful and sorrowful mysteries are usually wed together; if we fully experience one, we often feel the other. Perhaps you had many beautiful memories of your early life with your parents and siblings, and then you saw that happiness interrupted by parental fights that led to divorce and a broken home. When you remember the good times, you also remember what was lost. The same is true with painful memories; when we finally face the troubled times, we can be freed up to remember good times.

As I mentioned earlier in this book, my early life was tumultuous. I had two parents who loved me dearly and doted on me, especially in my early years. But my father's paranoid schizophrenia meant he could be scary, bizarre, and hostile when his illness held sway. In contrast, when his illness went into remission, he was the perfect father.

As I also mentioned early on, my grandparents' cabin that overlooked the swirling Chattahoochee was a solace for me. Related to the Ywahoo family of Cherokees, our family had been one in which many of the old traditions had been handed down. My grandfather had a near supernatural peacefulness about him. He would sing me soothing Native American chants that pierced my young heart with the infusion of the soothing and the sacred.

There were years when I was in grammar school when Daddy's illness was in remission and we delighted in doing things like fishing together and playing with my electric train. Daddy told me stories of how Pop's mother, his grandmother, a North Carolina Cherokee, taught him how to hunt with stone tipped arrows as well as how her herbs and chants could make sick people well.

Then when I was ten, Daddy's illness returned and he became more frightening and dangerous than before. When Daddy was ill, I had to listen to his bizarre delusions, listen to him yell at me that I was worthless, and hear his fears that the rest of the family was plotting to kill him.

My grandparents were my solace and strength. Then things got worse. When I was twelve, Pop's colon cancer, which had been operated on several years before, reemerged to carry him toward suffering and death. This was at a time when I spent half of each school day with my grandparents: they took care of me when my junior high was on half days due to overcrowding.

It was a comfort to be with them those half days, but gradually that comfort turned into overwhelming anxiety as Pop's cancer worsened and he lost weight quickly. I remember one scene when a lesion in his throat caused blood to trickle out of the side of his mouth.

It was all overwhelming. My grandfather, with whom I had shared sacred and safe times, was in excruciating pain and was soon to leave me. At the same time, my dad's mental illness held full sway.

A tsunami of dread and hopelessness surrounded me. I was in the scariest time of my life, and I no longer had anyone I could turn to for solace or understanding.

So I stopped feeling at all. I kept telling myself Pop wouldn't die; he might be sick, but he couldn't die. I stopped feeling, I stopped caring, and my insides turned to ice.

The time came when Pop could no longer sit up in the living room. Granny called Daddy at work. He came and carried Pop to his bed. This was the last time I saw Pop alive.

He lived on for a month, suffering greatly, but I did not have the courage to visit him in the bedroom. I could not see him dying. I could not see him writhing in pain. During that month, Pop often asked for me to come in the room and visit him, but I no longer had the courage.

The night he died, I gathered with the extended family in the kitchen of the cottage, where we kept vigil. Then screams pierced the silence as Granny and his older granddaughters wailed when he breathed his last breath. As I sat on the porch of the cottage, I saw the funeral home people wheel Pop out of the house on a gurney covered over by a sheet.

After that moment, I no longer thought of Pop. I no longer remembered. I struggled with my cerebral disability, and school was very hard for me. It was all too overwhelming, too much for me.

When I was thirteen, Daddy threatened to kill my mother and me and then showed up at our house with a gun. I rushed my mother out of the house and fled to a neighbor's home three blocks away. Daddy's frightening mental illness stayed the same for two years, and then went into remission, nearly for the rest of his life. He became a nurturing father. His new-found strength and gentleness became a solace for me, and no father could be as proud of a child as he was of me.

But my insides stayed shrunken. I no longer noticed or thought of Native Americans. Why should so much attention be shown to such backward people?

In my mid-twenties, I had a vivid dream of being carried by a whirlwind to the bluff where I stood with Pop as a child as he sang sacred chants. Nameless terror gripped my insides. I wanted to be anywhere but there. As an adult, I passed by the turn-off to their old house. I placed my hand by my right eye to block my vision of where their little home had stood.

There was a world full of memories I feared remembering. That repressed anxiety and guilt would erupt in my present as nameless fears and failing to warm up to people as readily as I would have liked. A barrier kept me from fully experiencing joy. Something huge in my life was missing and it caused me to distrust the sacred wonder of the present moment.

I knew I had to do something. As frightening as it might be, I needed to remember. I asked my father to talk to me about Pop. Daddy talked at length about his father and how he was a fortress of strength. He delighted in the Native American heritage we all had held together with Pop. He enchanted me with memories of his grandmother, Mary Elizabeth Alexander Ensley, Pop's mother.

I located great aunts, older relatives who remembered Pop and his mother. I sat at their feet as they told me stories of the old times.

I had to go back to the mountains in North Carolina where Pop was born and raised. I found the cabin he was born and partly reared in. I could barely look at the old house because of the tears that blinded my eyes. I collapsed into deep rhythmic sobs as two friends held me upright. Loss poured through me.

I had finally faced Pop's death and loss. With that came a letting go of guilt for not stepping into the room in which he was dying. I realized I had been carrying a Grand Canyon of guilt for, in my mind, abandoning him because I was scared. After I started to get in touch with those feelings, the healing process could begin. As I slowly came to see, the Pop I knew would understand the fear of the little boy I was.

Healing is a long process that, in a more subdued way, is still going on. For years after, I would break down every time I saw scenes of a little boy with his grandfather on television. I would even feel the loss and pain when I heard spoken Cherokee.

But for all the pain from the past, brightness lay open before me. Now I felt safe to remember all the amazing things about Pop that had so molded my life. I rediscovered my Native heritage. I knew that my penchant for contemplative prayer had come from Pop. I even remembered some of the songs he had taught me. I realized that my affinity for the great Christian heritage of contemplation and a deep walk with God came from Pop modeling quiet prayer and contemplation when I was young. My love for the Christian spiritual tradition came from Pop and his silences. He was a wonderful example of living in the present moment and loving Jesus and the Scriptures.

I was making peace with the past. I had to face the trauma I experienced growing up at home with my mother and father, reliving the terror and sheer loneliness of it again. This process was slow and is one that is still going on; but facing both the good and hurtful things from the past has brought wholeness to my life. I found a reservoir of strength and joy in my depths, where God resides. I found it much easier to love. I witnessed my soul develop a compassion for the pain of humanity and all creation that only making peace with the past can bring.

Sometimes when we worry constantly, it means we have failed to experience and face a sorrow that we felt at an earlier period in our lives. Worry becomes a defense against feeling past loss. The children we once were are still within us. We carry the hurts of childhood deep in us. We can pray for our pasts as well as our present and our future. And while we can't remake the past, we can bring Jesus into the past.

⟩ TIME FOR CALMING PRAYER ⟨

A Prayer ❋ *Dear Jesus, you had a past—not only from your birth and growing up years but from your heritage as a Jew. Your ancestors walked through the parted sea through a great act of God's deliverance. You led the Jewish people through tender chords of love. This is a heritage of great good, and you embraced that heritage.*

You walked beside us when we did not even know you were there. You were with us when life bruised us and wore us down. You see how strains from the past are such a powerful, often hidden influence on the present.

Dear Lord, we open up to you the pages of our past. Heal the little children we once were. Soothe the hurts that have accompanied us for a lifetime. Heal the scars. Help us to let go of all harmful worry, whether from the past or the present. For you are indeed the healer, the comforter, and restorer of our souls. Free us to remember the good things, the times we were loved and cherished, our early accomplishments, and our family's heritage. Amen.

Scripture Reflection ❀

For I am sure that neither death, nor life, nor angels, nor principalities, nor things present, nor things to come, nor powers, nor height, nor depth, nor anything else in all creation, will be able to separate us from the love of God in Christ Jesus our Lord.   ROMANS 8:38–39, RSV

Guided Meditation ❀

You walk into a room in a beautiful home. Filled with comfortable furniture and vividly green plants, it is a room designed to relax you. You sit on a thick-padded couch. A picture window looks out over the ocean. The sound and sight of the waves breaking on the shore deeply still you. The waves remind you of the rhythms of God's love that can flow over you, just like the sea flows over the beach. Relax there a moment.

You hear sounds of sandals clip-clopping over the tiled floor. You turn and see Jesus walking toward you in his sandals and robe. He asks if he may sit with you and you say yes. He holds your hand and you feel a rush of love and calm flow from his hand to your hand. From your hand, the loving calm fills your body and soul. You sit with him a moment.

He says to you, "I want to take you on a walk through the past." He pulls you up and leads you down a hall. You come to a door with the sign, "Joyful Memories from the Past." Jesus leads you into the room. It is filled with joyful scenes from your childhood. The pictures are brightly lit.

Your eye goes to a particularly joyful picture. You feel the feelings of those times. Rejoice again at those memories.

Perhaps seeing a joyful scene brings feelings of pain and loss as well. Jesus leads you back to the couch and asks you what negative feelings you may have felt, what painful scenes might have emerged. He puts his arm around your shoulder and the presence of his love slowly heals the wounded child within you.

CHAPTER SEVEN

Making Peace with Fear and Anxiety

Fear and anxiety are those unpleasant sensations that many of us know all too well: a tight feeling in the chest or stomach with perhaps a tinge of nausea, a choking feeling in the throat, rapid heartbeat, and perhaps a little sweating, all in anticipation of some real or perceived danger. We feel overwhelmed. We anticipate the worst. Fear and anxiety may come in the form of anything from a moderate discomfort to a full-fledged panic attack.

The word fear comes from the Old English *faer* which means a sudden danger. This type of fear is often easily justified. When an uncontrolled car barrels toward you as you are driving, fear serves a critical purpose. It startles you to maneuver out of the way. Being fearful of driving in dangerous conditions can be a good fear, causing us to slow down and drive more carefully. If you see your child about to cross the street without looking, the fear impels you to firmly take hold of the child to prevent a catastrophe. This type of fear is of great help if you are to avoid harm whenever possible.

What usually haunts us is not this helpful kind of fear, but fear that is out of control. Often we call this type of fear anxiety. The Latin root of *anxious* means a constricted tight feeling in the chest. This kind of fear stays with us even when there is no immediate danger. Worry and dread fill us, and often there appears to be no cause for the fear. It most often comes when we are haunted by the "what ifs" of life.

Fear and anxiety can become so entrenched that they can be categorized as a disorder or illness: a disorder that abounds in the twenty-first century. The National Institute of Mental Health tells us that around twenty percent of adults are diagnosed with an anxiety disorder. That translates into twenty million adults, not to mention many millions more who are undiagnosed.[17] There are also those whose lives are inhibited by a level of anxiety and fear that does not rise to the level of diagnosable disorder.

The gospels contain one hundred twenty-six commands of Christ. Of these commands, the highest number command is to not be afraid, to not be anxious, to take heart, or to take courage. This is even more times than the second most common demand, to love God and to love neighbor, which is mentioned eight times. Yet, we often worry about things that are in the future.

Sometimes the fear that menaces us is as real as our hands and feet. For instance, the doctor discovers fast-moving cancer in your spouse and tells you your loved one has only two months at best. Perhaps the manufacturing plant that employs you announces it is closing, or you get served with divorce papers.

Jesus knew fear, the scariest kind of fear, as he encountered a real worst-case scenario. He faced capture, mockery, lashes with a whip full of glass shards, and merciless torture on a cross. This wasn't a fear blown out of proportion; it was as real as his heartbeat or his breath.

Jesus did two things to deal with that anxiety. As *The Message* version puts it: "He plunged into a sinkhole of dreadful agony" (Mark 14:33). First, he faced it. Second, he prayed. In the Garden of Gethsemane, Jesus faced the ultimate fear with a raw and authentic prayer, "Abba, Father," he cried out, "everything is possible for you. Please take this cup of suffering away from me. Yet I want your will to be done, not mine" (Mark 14:36).

Torture and death were not the last word for Jesus. Resurrection came on the third day. And resurrection can come for us. Awareness of God's triumph over all our worst-case scenarios can touch us even in the midst of that sinkhole of dreadful agony. As the psalmist tells us, "Weeping may last for the night, but joy comes with the morning" (Psalm 30:5).

Like Jesus, we can face our fear and anxiety, beg God that we not drink of suffering, and tell him of the horror. With the help of the Spirit, we can pray, "Not my will but yours be done."

When fear haunts us, our reaction can easily be to have our souls curl up in a fetal position. Dread becomes our food and drink. As Max Lucado suggests, we make a god out of "safety, we worship the risk free life."[18] When our souls are brimful of fear, constantly searching for safety, we can find it really difficult to care for the poor and hurting, the environment, the least among us, or fulfill the purposes of our lives. We can't be content. When we worship safety, we will find out we can't do great and wonderful things for God and others. To love means to risk, and if we cannot risk, we cannot love deeply or hope or dream with abandon—all of which are essential to the life of the believer. The worship of safety ultimately leads to dehumanization.

The answer for this kind of fear, this anxiety, is to be rearranged inside, to allow the Spirit to give us fresh identities: identities as God's own children, loved and enabled to live, by his love. Paul sums this up when he writes: "You did not receive the spirit of slavery to fall back into but you have received the spirit of sonship" (Romans 8:15).

Erik Erikson wrote that the essential need of babies is trust. When you really think about it, it is the basic need for adults too. The best way for adults to learn to trust is to lean back on safe and everlasting arms. As we taste God's love for us over and over again, trust is born in us. According to Fulton Sheen, "Anxiety increases in direct proportion as a person departs from God."[19]

I especially remember Ella, a middle-aged woman I met while giving a retreat. An English professor at a nearby college, she had clawed her way from near destitution to a professional role in life.

At times in her early life, she experienced love and received at least some of the hugs and pats on the back that all of us need when we are growing up. Her father fled from his responsibilities and abandoned Ella, an only child, and her mother when she was three. At first her mother, who had dropped out of high school when she became pregnant with Ella, did her best. She worked the only jobs available to her: working at a car-wash or a fast-food restaurant for minimum pay. They lived in crime-ridden public housing. But even with food stamps they had no food for supper. Ella was well acquainted with hunger and clothed with rescue mission clothes.

In her despair, her mother turned to alcohol and kept losing jobs because of being under the influence at work. Her mother gave Ella hugs and kisses, but not much else. Finally, in a drunken rage, her mother got into a fight with the woman who lived in the neighboring apartment. The police were called, saw the condition of the mother and child, and then called in child protective services. Because of the neglect, barren cupboards, and alcoholism, the state removed Ella from the home. A few months later, her inebriated mother was killed when she meandered into the path of an oncoming truck as she walked along the highway.

Life was not good for Ella in the foster homes. No one abused her, but no one loved her either. The three sets of foster parents took her in because of the money paid to them by the state, not because they wanted more children. However, her mother had made sure she attended Mass each weekend and through her times with foster parents she kept this up. The church was the one steadying force in her life.

Ella fiercely wanted to break out of all of this. Blessed with an IQ in the upper regions, she shone at school. From the time she went into foster care at twelve, she studied late into the night to achieve outstanding grades. Despite lack of love and lack of resources, she determined that school would be her way out. Her hard work was rewarded. She was valedictorian of her graduating class, and a nearby university offered her a generous academic scholarship.

Even the good scholarship didn't cover everything, however, and she had to take a part-time job to earn her bachelor's degree and later her master's and doctorate. She fought for her diplomas with all her might.

After earning her doctorate, she was hired to teach literature at a community college. She lived a life shaped by fear: fear she would fail at teaching and fear she would lose her health and be brought back to destitution. She held high expectations of her students. It terrified her to think that, unlike her, her students would fail to study and not excel. She had worked hard to achieve so much, and she counted on the same from her students. She had little patience with students she labeled as slackers: students who had a difficult time with the course work for whatever reason. She flew into rages with them. She had achieved despite terrible circumstances, and they could too! She often wrote phrases in red on papers such as "incompetent" and "shameful." She humiliated them in front of other students. Even an A- was not good enough for her students. Without realizing it, she was abusing them.

Her fear developed into an even worse rage toward her students. A student who had cognitive deficits and epilepsy due to a closed head injury in a car wreck became a target of Ella's anger. He was bright, but his motor skills were affected, and it was nearly impossible for him to take accurate class notes. Despite his struggles, he maintained a B average in all his courses, except hers where he was limping along with a C. It was the day when cassette recorders were still in use and he often used one to record the lectures he could not take notes on. One day, early in the course, he asked if he could record her since he had a hard time taking notes. Ella blew up at him. Losing control she yelled, "You think you deserve special treatment because you consider yourself a 'crip'? I made it without any help in conditions far worse than you will ever know. Stop avoiding work and take notes just like everyone else."

The distraught young man left the class in tears. Left with few options, he filed a civil rights complaint with the dean and the administration. The administration circled the wagons around Ella, their peer, but the young man could not leave it at that. He had to find some way to take the course. In desperation he turned to an attorney friend of his family, who filed a complaint for him with the civil rights division of the justice department. They decided to intervene with mediation.

At the mediation everyone listened to the words Ella had spewed out at him in class, thanks to a recording another student had secretly made. The reality of the abuse hit Ella and the administration like a sudden plunge into cold water. The mediator did not mince words. "The teacher is out of line here. This situation needs to be changed." At that moment everyone, even Ella, realized things could not continue the way they had been.

"How could I have been so cruel?" Ella said. Then looking at the young man, she apologized with a cracking voice, "I am so sorry."

The attorney for the young man took him to a nearby room and conferred with him. Then he and the attorney for the school talked quietly. The man's attorney spoke to the gathered group. "My client is grateful the instructor realized her mistake and we don't want to see her terminated. We would like her to give permission for my client to use the recorder and for the instructor to accommodate his disability in other reasonable ways, such as more time on tests. Finally, we want her to seek psychotherapy to work on her communication skills and the way she treats students." Ella and the school agreed to all this.

Psychotherapy, with a devout Catholic psychotherapist, was the beginning of her redemption. The first thing he told her was that fear keeps us locked in on the past and the future, not living in the present moment.

As Ella talked about her past she realized her terror that her students might falter or fail came from the fears that embedded themselves in her during her painful childhood and teen years. The psychotherapist urged her to look squarely at her fears and acknowledge them when they came up. Ella learned that prayer and meditation could be of great help.

She came to realize that there was a wounded child within her crying out for help. In a guided meditation, the psychotherapist helped her meet that wounded child, with Jesus standing by the adult Ella's side. She imagined taking Jesus to meet the scrawny, ill-clad child. In her imagination, Jesus embraced her and the wounded child at the same time saying, "You have no need to fear. I and Ella are always here to comfort you and help you come to peace." Ella mussed up the hair of the wounded child and said, "You are no longer alone. Jesus and I are always with you."

Ella breathed a profound sigh of peace and relief. Acknowledging her fearful child and taking that child to Jesus for comfort and well-being marked the first step in Ella's coming to peace. There would be many more therapy sessions and meetings with Jesus in meditation, but Ella found her peace and, as a result of the process, now excelled in the way she treated her students.

⥤ TIME FOR CALMING PRAYER ⥢

Scripture Reflection—Do not be afraid ❀ Let's pause
and move to praying now. Slowly, prayerfully, savoring each
word, meditate on some of those Scriptures:

> Peace I leave with you; my peace I give to you. I do
> not give to you as the world gives. Do not let your
> hearts be troubled, and do not let them be afraid.
> JOHN 14:27

> He said to them, "Why are you frightened, and why
> do doubts arise in your hearts? Look at my hands
> and my feet; see that it is I myself. Touch me and
> see." LUKE 24:38–39A

> And you will hear of wars and rumors of wars; see
> that you are not alarmed. MATTHEW 24:6A

> But Jesus came and touched them, saying, "Get up
> and do not be afraid." MATTHEW 17:7

> Don't let your hearts be troubled. Trust in God,
> and trust also in me....I will come and get you,
> so that you will always be with me where I am.
> JOHN 14:1, 3 (NLT)

A Prayer ❀ *Lord, the immensity of your love shines through
the ordinary, daily things of life. Help us to notice the little ways
you come to us each moment. You have seeded the everyday
things of life with your immortality. May we delight in the small*

things that carry the taste of eternity. We unlatch the gates of our hearts so that your healing may calm our fear, right here, right now. Now, Lord, open us to your touch. Open us to your leading that we may spend ourselves in compassion for your world. Amen.

Guided Meditation ❃

Sit in a chair; put an empty chair near you.

Close your eyes. Imagine you are the hurt, fearful child of your past. Feel the loneliness and any terror that may be there. Put it into the child's words. "I am so scared people will leave me; so scared I will die wounded by the harsh words of parents, peers, and others. I just don't think I can make it on my own."

Now, go sit in the other chair and be your adult self.

Gently, Jesus comes and stands beside you, placing his arm on your shoulder. You feel the ease of his love pass through you. Fear and tension slip away at his touch. You stand up and Jesus takes your hand and walks you over to the frightened child you once were. The child stands up and Jesus envelops the two of you in a comforting embrace. He says to the wounded child, "Dear one, you are not alone. I have been with you since before you were born. Always let me touch you, for my touch will bring the deepest peace. I am always with you."

Then you say to the child comforting words like this, "You are no longer alone. We made it through. I will take care of you. I will let you weep on my shoulder when you need to weep, and I'll embrace you when you need embracing. Let me guide you and you will become strong."

Jesus now spreads his hands over you and the child. He blesses you. Light streaming from his wounded palms cascades over the two of you. You breathe the light in, letting it drench you both in and out as it washes away fear with an eternity of caring.

CHAPTER EIGHT

Making Peace with Anger

It came as no surprise to Andrew that his wife, Iris, might be facing at least some jail time. After slapping down another woman whose car had rammed into hers, she was booked on assault charges. With further investigation, there was the possibility they would be raised to felony assault. No one was hurt in the accident, but there were some scratches and dented places on the bumper. The other motorist had been following her too close and probably been daydreaming.

"How dare she do that!" Iris thought. In a fury, she stormed over to the open window where the other woman sat at the wheel. She reached in, uttering a stream of profanity, and started shaking and slapping the woman, leaving some scratches. When the police arrived and took her statement, Iris blamed the other motorist, letting go another stream of profanities. The officer then stepped over to talk to the other woman. Glee raced through her body as she saw the motorist being ticketed.

The officer then stepped back to Iris saying, "The other motorist was at fault, but nothing justifies your use of violence toward her. I am arresting you for assault." Protests didn't help, and soon Iris found herself in the back of the squad car, hand-cuffed and headed for jail.

When Andrew was informed, he actually breathed a sigh of relief that his wife had not pulled out the handgun under the seat and done far more harm. Andrew loved his wife. She could be charming, full of laughter and compassion. But she possessed a hair-trigger temper and had verbally attacked him and their thirteen-year-old daughter many times. She would soon get over it and return to her normal, caring self. He thought losing her job as a high school teacher a few months before, because of conflicts she initiated with students, faculty, and the principal, would teach her a lesson.

He bailed her out. They were silent till they got home. When they were finally seated together in the den, he calmly asked her what happened.

"It was not my fault. If she had not been such a horrible driver and hit my car, I would have been fine. She made me so mad. You know my anger rarely lasts more than a minute. I vent and then it is over with."

Andrew replied to her, "So is a shotgun. Like your temper, it's over in a minute too, but it blows everything to bits."

When he said that, Iris raged, "You always take the other person's point of view. You don't believe me; you never have." She began pummeling Andrew's chest with soft, half-hearted blows.

Andrew, instead of responding in kind, enveloped her in a full, tight, warmhearted embrace. She finally stopped accusing him and collapsed into his arms where her accusations turned into deep sobs. After a few minutes weeping in his arms, she said contritely, "I can't help myself. I need help."

Andrew, still embracing her, said, "Know that I love you and I always will. We can get through this together."

She finally agreed to enter an anger management program and seek further help through a psychotherapist with Catholic social services. She had given up God and stopped going to church after she was dismissed from her job at the high school. Now, she started going back to church, accompanying her husband and daughter. She joined a contemplative prayer group in her parish, allowing God's love, in prayer, to touch her inside, where her anger was gradually transformed into compassion.

She pleaded guilty to the charges, showed remorse, and was sentenced to three years strict probation, as long as she got individual therapy and was in an anger management class.

Anger can be a force to mobilize to defend the weak and confront injustice. For instance, when Jesus cleansed the temple, throwing out the tax collectors, or Lech Walesa confronted Communism in Poland, they were exhibiting a righteous anger. Anger is like fire; properly channeled it can light a candle; unchecked it can burn down half of Southern California through unhindered forest fires. In this chapter, we are talking about the destructive form of anger that is often fueled by poor self-esteem.

So how do we handle anger? Suppressing anger is not a good

option. When we turn anger inward, it can become destructive causing depression, anxiety disorders, high blood pressure, and susceptibility to heart disease. Neither is it a good idea to vent our anger on another person. Dumping our unchecked anger directly on others can lead to hostility, damage our relationships, and spill over to all of our emotions, leaving us flooded with negativity.

How do we respond when others get angry at us? It's easy to respond with anger, to react by having the same emotion we are confronted with. Anger gives birth to anger. Venting at one another is not a good path to follow.

Perhaps someone's angry words hurt us. We tend to say to others, "Look at what he (or she) did to me! Can you believe it?" We hold on to hostility, letting anger draw us back to an unpleasant past. Such anger can so tie us up inside we don't have the energy to enjoy the here and now or feel the subtle nudges of God in our hearts. This state of emotion hurts us, not the other person.

Someone may stimulate or trigger our anger. It's all the other person's fault! This person is responsible for the way I feel. We point fingers. In this case, we are reacting rather than acting. If we look closely, we may find that much of our anger comes from our reaction rather than what someone said or did to us. If we examine the patterns of emotion in our lives, the anger may be larger than whatever was said or done to us.

When we give into animosity and rage we find that it is ourselves whom we destroy. St. Paul writes:

> Let no evil talk come out of your mouths, but only
> what is useful for building up, as there is need, so

that your words may give grace to those who hear. And do not grieve the Holy Spirit of God, with which you were marked with a seal for the day of redemption. Put away from you all bitterness and wrath and anger and wrangling and slander, together with all malice, and be kind to one another, tender-hearted, forgiving one another, as God in Christ.

EPHESIANS 4:29–32

Don't vent your anger on another but accept it. Feel it as an emotion that will pass through us and out of us if we do not cling to it. An Arab proverb states: "Anger is a wind that blows out the lamp of the mind." As author Madelin Adena Smith phrases it, "Forget feeling afraid of anger, forget tempering your emotions. Feel them; but when you do; remember that these emotions belong to you and only you."[20]

It is easy to assume that active Christians shouldn't get angry. Sister Emily Meisel, who leads one-on-one sessions as well as group sessions on handling anger at the Benedictine Spirituality Center at Sacred Heart Monastery in Richardton, South Dakota, says: "It takes an awful lot of energy to hang on to anger and resentment." Processing our anger means "we're a more whole and happy person, and that's what God wants for us." Meisel states it simply. Anger is "an awareness that something is wrong."[21]

Very often an underlying emotion is under the anger. For some reason, some people do not like themselves and have poor self-esteem. Anger often is merely the tip of the iceberg. It is secondary to those underlying emotions, like the rest of the iceberg that lies unseen beneath the surface.

Here are some things we can do when dealing with anger.

1. Notice the physical signs of anger such as a knotted stomach, a heavily beating heart, or sweat on your palms.
2. Deal with habits of anger when they are small, before they become entrenched.
3. Actively acknowledge the emotion of anger. This is an essential step in getting a grip on our lives.
4. Take the feelings to God in prayer. Name the reasons for anger to God one at a time. Yell them out to God if you need to.
5. Look within to try to find the origins of your anger. Get at the root of it.
6. Journal about the emotion of anger or talk to a therapist or trained spiritual director.
7. Make it concrete, physical. Pound your fist on a pillow to let out the emotion. Throw yourself into yard work, vigorously pulling out weeds, for instance. Some find playing or hitting on a drum a way to let go of anger.
8. Seek professional help if the roots of the anger grow deep within you or you are dealing with issues of low self-esteem or self-loathing.

Contemplative style prayer, simply resting in the love of God, is one of the best helps in dealing with anger. It is letting God do what he wants to do: simply love us.

When we surround our inner emotions with the love that pours from God into our heart, anger is transformed. Just as the sunshine takes care of vegetation, so prayer can transform our inmost feelings. The light of the sun pierces flower buds so deeply that at some point they cannot resist; they just have to open up in full bloom. When we saturate our emotions with the kind of prayer that opens us to the nurture of an everlasting love, it can transform what is within us.

Anger is like cut-up raw potatoes. Raw potatoes are inedible, but if we boil them for thirty minutes we are met with the luscious smell of cooked potatoes, just ready to eat. So it is with anger. If we take thirty minutes to saturate it with the warmth of the love of God, anger can be transformed to understanding and compassion.

One way of opening our insides to God's love is to repeat a shortened version of the Jesus Prayer, "Jesus, Lord Jesus" very softly, at least moving our lips. Repeating the rhythm of that name calms and stills us, opening up our hearts to God. Don't worry about wandering thoughts; everyone has them, even Jesus because he was human. When you notice your mind wandering, simply return to saying the prayer. If in thirty minutes of praying in this manner, your mind wanders a hundred times and you return to saying your prayer, you have made one hundred acts of loving God. Some find this form of prayer so soothing they feel as refreshed as having slept a good night's sleep.

The Rosary is also a phenomenal contemplative pathway. The Rosary is a surprising and excellent way to let God revamp the insides of our soul and to enable us to exchange our anger for understanding.

⇒ TIME FOR CALMING PRAYER ⇐

Scripture reflection ❀

The Lord passed before him, and proclaimed, "The Lord, the Lord, a God merciful and gracious, slow to anger, and abounding in steadfast love and faithfulness." EXODUS 34:6

Put away from you all bitterness and wrath and anger and wrangling and slander, together with all malice, and be kind to one another, tender-hearted, forgiving one another, as God in Christ has forgiven you. Therefore be imitators of God, as beloved children, and live in love, as Christ loved us and gave himself up for us, a fragrant offering and sacrifice to God. EPHESIANS 4:31—5:2

A Prayer ❀ *Dear Lord, you have shown each of us countless mercies. If we let it, your mercy can sink into the very fiber of our being. You put your wrath away and embrace us instead.*

Show us how to show mercy instead of rage, and empathy instead of wrangling. As you work your work of change within us, change self-righteousness into humility. Give us listening hearts and listening ears that help us hear the cries of the heart of those nearby us who enrage us, and to go deeper and listen to the inner heartbeat of others rather than their outward behavior. Teach us the difference between anger that tears apart and anger that defends and protects.

Guided Meditation ❈ Let God's stillness settle over you. Play some soothing instrumental music or nature sounds to remind you of the soothing touch of God's Spirit.

Jesus comes and stands beside you. He places his hand on your chest, calming your heart within.

He tells you, "I hear some rumbling in your heart, your anger. In the safety of my presence pour out your ire, railing, shouting, crying to me. Anytime your indignation rises in your heart, tell me without hesitation, leaving it at the only place it should be left, my feet."

CHAPTER NINE

Making Peace with Suffering

When I think of suffering, I think of Jean, a middle-aged woman I met at a Weight Watchers meeting when I was still a very young man. Just from being with her, I spotted the look of God's nearness in her eyes and face and a touch of God's own voice in her voice. Not fully understanding why, I knew I was in the presence of holiness.

Jean was partially paralyzed from rheumatoid arthritis. She walked with a cane, and her fingers were curled. One night she asked me to go out for coffee after the meeting. Over coffee, her story unfolded. She had been a successful executive secretary until her illness hit. Then she had to go on disability.

While her seventy-eight-year-old mother stood by her, her siblings pushed her aside, not willing to be near the scariness of her situation. Despite all this, she spoke often of how uplifting the services at her Baptist church were and how much she loved reading the Bible. We made a regular plan of going out for coffee after each meeting and talking about God and how faithful he is. Despite her suffering, it was clear that a bright inner joy burned within her. She laughed easily and just as easily showed me empathy and love in my own trials.

Then a few weeks before the new year she asked Deacon Robert and me if we could celebrate New Year's with her in her apartment. Her voice broke as she told me why. Many years before when she was still young, her husband abandoned her on New Year's Eve, announcing his intent to divorce her. She needed friends to be with her on that evening. The two of us readily agreed. The three of us had a glorious New Year's Eve at her apartment, drinking soda, and celebrating the occasion eating food frowned on by Weight Watchers. For many years, New Year's with Jean became a regular event to look forward to.

Then one summer her mother called to tell me that Jean had been diagnosed with terminal cancer. I rushed over to see her. As she lay in her hospital room bed, I saw a look of sheer horror and panic on her face. Silently I asked, "Why, God? Why? Why should something this terrible happen to someone who was so good?" All I could do was be present to Jean as she lay in her hospital bed.

The days and months rolled by and Jean's disease progressed to its last stages. Another call came from Jean's mother. Jean was stuck in a chair and could not get up. She asked if Robert and I could help move her.

When we arrived at their home, Jean was sitting in a chair, alert and conscious, but barely able to speak. Her eyes welcomed us. I embraced her as much as I was able with her sitting stiffly in the chair. As I leaned over, the crucifix around my neck dangled out from my chest. Jean, slowly and painfully pulled herself toward the crucifix, fingered the corpus, then kissed it and mouthed, "Thank you."

All I can say is that she clung to Christ and that "old rugged cross" as the song from the Baptist hymnal says. She joined her sufferings with Christ's and his with hers. This was the only answer to my troubled question of "Why?" This side of glory, that is the only explanation we have.

Jean died several days later. I thanked God I had the honor of taking her from her chair to the bed. As I mentioned earlier, when I was thirteen I watched my father carry my grandfather from his chair to his bedroom for the last time. At that time, my soul was frightened into ice. I avoided ever entering Pop and Granny's bedroom and seeing Pop again before he died. This time, I was the one who took Jean to her bed for the last time. Before, out of fear, I had run from Pop's suffering. Now, I embraced Jean's. Only God's grace made that possible.

Suffering, loneliness, and devastation may seem like mysteries that cannot be fathomed. No amount of money or earthly pleasure can inoculate us from them. Even faith cannot protect us from suffering.

All our thinking and rational thought cannot penetrate the mystery of suffering. As Fr. Michael Heinrich has written:

> This mystery is one that is only solved by the Cross...
> The cross is the *Incarnational* moment where love

and suffering meet. Love because "God is love" (1 Jn 4:16b) and suffering because the human condition is deeply affected by sin and death (Gen 3:16ff). Christ took upon himself the entirety of our human condition. While this expressed itself in his person I believe it was brought to completion by his sacrifice. It was only in his death that he was able to "reconcile to himself all things, whether on earth or in heaven, making peace *through* the blood of his cross" (Col 1:20).[22]

A story I once heard beautifully illustrates all this. Once there was a magnificent king who ruled over a large realm. He lived in an elegant castle set high above the valley. The finest music and food were to be had in that castle. The king's robes glittered with gold and jewels. The sounds of joy and laughter filled the building.

In the valley below, people lived in poverty, squalor, and violence. They yearned for the merriment and ease found in the castle above. There wasn't enough food, and there wasn't enough love. Suffering, frightened, and nearly without hope, the people of the valley lived out their lives of desperation.

Then one day the king told his tailors that he wanted fresh clothes. They presented him with new gorgeous finery. He said no to their creation; it was not what he wanted.

Finally, in exasperation, he told them he would make the clothes himself. He went into a room to sew them for several days. When he emerged, he was wearing shabby and cheap clothes, not fit for any king.

Startled, his entourage asked him why. He said he wanted to dress like his people in the valley. In fact, he was going down to the valley to live with the people there and share their suffering.

Every devout believer, who lives for the good of others and the glory of God, suffers in the suffering of all those to whom she or he ministers. If this is true of us, how much more must it be so for God?

Back in 1983, the son of William Sloane Coffin, the pastor of New York's famous Riverside Church, was killed in a car accident. As close friends and family comforted Sloane, one questioned whether this was the will of God or not. Coffin responded immediately that this was not the will of God. "The one thing that should never be said when someone dies is 'It is the will of God,'" Coffin said in the eulogy for his son Alex. "Never do we know enough to say that. My own consolation lies in knowing that it was not the will of God that Alex die; that when the waves closed over the sinking car, God's heart was the first of all our hearts to break."[23]

There are two kinds of suffering. The first is bodily suffering, which includes illness and physical pain. There is also mental and emotional suffering. Both types are felt in the body, either through pain or through the tightened tense muscles that mental and emotional suffering bring. That's why we need to slow down and give the body rest, taking time to pause and taste and smell the aroma of peace in creation.

We should not embrace suffering for suffering's sake. Modern culture gives us ways to avoid some suffering. Medical science now can offer healing for once incurable conditions. Counseling offers the possibilities of reconciliation in strained relationships and help for the inner storms we face.

Palliative care can ease the suffering of terminal illnesses.

We shouldn't turn our backs on such helps. Thanks to our modern culture there is some suffering we don't have to endure.

Still, there is suffering medical science cannot alleviate. And terminal illness, despite palliative care, still means death; and the people who are dying and those who love them suffer. When suffering cannot be avoided, it can be embraced.

And isn't there a third kind of suffering that is close to Jesus' heart? Suffering on behalf of others? How often do we shy away from being a person for others because of the suffering or hardship it might bring? And, of course there is suffering when we don't take time for our most important relationship, our relationship with God.

The problem is when our culture (never explicitly, but still really, if unconsciously) helps us think we can avoid all suffering and even death. The modern consumer culture tells us we'll be happy with the new house and car and be thrilled by the movie or sports event. And we, eager to never suffer at all or die, jump in.

Flowers need moist earth, mud, to grow and flourish. But mud can also stink. We need to learn to cultivate the sufferings we have to endure, like we cultivate mud for our plants. Joy, happiness, and compassion can flourish in suffering just as flowers flourish in the mud.

Rather than diverting our attention from our suffering, the way to handle suffering is to embrace it and cradle it tenderly, taking up our cross and bearing it just as Jesus took up his cross and embraced his suffering.

When we slow down and pray the name of Jesus with our breath, or slowly and tenderly repeat Hail Marys for a while, we become aware of the intensity of our suffering. It was begging for attention and now that we have given it attention, we can cling to the outstretched hand of God. He is so near us when we let suffering bring us into the mending that is his presence.

A mother can cradle her little baby in her arms when his or her distressing screams fill the room. She does this without judging or ignoring the baby's suffering. In the same way, we can cradle our own anguish, asking Jesus to stand with us and sing a lullaby.

Just as there is light in the darkest cloud, so there is a ray of heavenly hope in the greatest calamities. There is no misery so great, no sorrow so deep, and no trial so bitter that God cannot change it into a door of hope.

Think of the patient, long-suffering appeal that our Blessed Lord makes, bearing with all our weaknesses and defects. He does not allow his gentle hand to be turned away, even though the door has been so long barred and bolted to him. Let these sweet thoughts of a Christ that gives everything, of a Christ whose every dealing is filled with love, of a Christ who pleads with us through the barred door and tries to get to us through the obstacles that we ourselves have fastened against him, draw us to him, and kindle and keep alight a brighter flame of dedication and of devotion in our hearts to him.

⸺ TIME FOR CALMING PRAYER ⸺

A Prayer ❋ *Dear Lord, you walked the way of suffering, your* via dolorosa. *You drank to the last drop the cup of our humanity. You came from on high to live in the valley here below, in the valley with us, your fellow sufferers. You took on our sufferings, our loneliness, and our desperation. Help us to learn to entrust our suffering to you, to join our wounds with yours. On the cross, you spread your embrace to encircle the suffering of each one of us, the suffering of all creation.*

We undergo long-term sufferings: adult children who seem to have lost their way, depression, the loss of those we love, and many more calamities. May all sorrows ripen us, may they be a cord that binds us to you. Be with us when all the clouds are dark. May your calming, comforting, consoling ray of light break through, filling our hearts with your tender mercies.

Scripture Reflection ❋

Therefore, since we are justified by faith, we have peace with God through our Lord Jesus Christ, through whom we have obtained access to this grace in which we stand; and we boast in our hope of sharing the glory of God. And not only that, but we also boast in our sufferings, knowing that suffering produces endurance, and endurance produces character, and character produces hope, and hope does not disappoint us, because God's love has been poured into our hearts through the Holy Spirit that has been given to us.

For while we were still weak, at the right time Christ died for the ungodly. Indeed, rarely will anyone die for a righteous person—though perhaps for a good person someone might actually dare to die. But God proves his love for us in that while we still were sinners Christ died for us. ROMANS 5:1–8

....

Guided Meditation ❋ You are lying down in a beautiful meadow beside a large tree. You feel the warmth of the springtime's sun caress you. These rays are special rays; they are the rays of God's own love. His calming tenderness penetrates into the very muscles of your body, relaxing them, bringing peace to body and soul. The bright green grass gently holds you as you sink into relaxing quiet. You feel your stresses and strains pass through you into the air and the ground. Peace reigns in your soul. It is good to be there.

You hear the grass rustling. You look up and there is Jesus walking toward you. Your eyes lock with his and in his eyes you see an infinity of love. He motions for you to stand up. You do, and he quietly encircles you in his arms. The fire of the Spirit that lights his heart now lights your heart. Together you look out over the meadow and trees and a stream, which in his presence look luminescent with glory.

Now that you are safe and at peace with Jesus there beside you, Jesus asks you to name some of the ways in your life you have suffered. Perhaps you feel some of the feelings of being lost that come as you name them. Those feelings gather in your heart, pass through you out your arm and through your hand that clasps Jesus' wounded hand. They then travel into his hand, where they flow to disappear in the flame that is his sacred heart. You do the same with the suffering of those you love. Finally, you sense the pain of a wounded creation flow through you to your hand and into his heart. You look down and see that the hand that held Jesus' now has a wound like his and you have joined your wounds to his, hand in hand.

CHAPTER TEN

Making Peace with Death

There is a touching story about a young boy, sitting on a limb, trying to tie a leaf to the branch. An adult came by and asked the boy, "What are you doing?" The young boy replied that his sister was very, very ill. She was near death, and the doctor had told his family that "ere the last leaf shall fall from the tree in the front yard, she will be gone." The little boy didn't want her to die, so he was tying the leaves back on the trees as if that could spare his sister's life.[24]

One of the most common fears people face is the fear of death. It is part of xenophobia, the fear of the unknown. We may fear poor health, but usually there is something we can do about it. We can exercise, eat a diet that's healthy and nutritious, and avoid habits like drinking too much. On one level, we can get a handle on it. If we fear public speaking, we can avoid speaking in public or build up our confidence. So it goes with most of our other fears. However, this does not apply to death. We have never died; it is a big unknown, but we know that we will die. The grim reaper comes for all of us without exception. It is difficult, near impossible, to get a handle on it.

We may be people of faith, but deep down we may fear that death is nothingness. Or, if we were raised in a particularly negative religious environment, we may fear hell and punishment.

The acceptance we talked about in an earlier chapter can help us, with Christ hand in hand with us, facing what seems to us a grim reality.

Tom was a healthy young friend of mine in New England. One day, he bent over with abdominal pain and nausea, having no idea of the source of his discomfort. Further tests gave him the worst possible news. He had advanced and terminal pancreatic cancer. He had a wonderful young wife and a five-year-old son. There was no life insurance; he had always thought of himself as too healthy for that. He envisioned his wife and child bankrupt and destitute after his death. Both he and his wife were inconsolable. Genuine fear and anxiety ruled his life.

He visited a healing service in search of a miracle. While God does at times work miraculously, no miracle came to heal him of his cancer. Anguish became his food and drink as he sank into a deep pit of despair. He tried to pray, using the prayers of his childhood, but the prayers seemed to not even rise up to the ceiling. In his mind God had abandoned him and his family. He thought he was losing his faith as well as his life. Fear gripped him like an iron hand squeezing his heart.

His pastor counseled him to read the gospel scenes of Jesus' agony in the garden and to find a time when he was alone in his house to scream out his torment to God, out loud in high volume, and then ask God to take his cup away. After two weeks of doing this, his screams turned to calm as he felt the touch of Abba Father. Finally, he prayed, "Not my will but yours be done." He felt the everlasting arms embrace him.

As much as he could, he lived each day for the day. There was suffering, but he began to cherish his family as never before, making each moment a time to reach out in love and receive love. His wife gave him the news that a local school district had hired her to teach English for the upcoming year, a reality that eased his financial concerns. He felt his heart warm with the awareness of God's love as it came to him in silence and prayer, nature, and others. In his last days, his love and courage affected many. He died a peaceful death.

In pastoral counseling classes and in ministry, we are asked not to sugarcoat death. People face a harsh reality, and it is best that we simply stand by them in their anguish, to let the natural process of letting go play its role. This is indeed wise advice. In considering our own deaths and the death of those we love, we need to grieve well. Yet as people of faith it is also true, as St. Paul reminds us, that we do not grieve as those who have no hope. As Christ said, "I am the resurrection and the life. Those who believe in me, even though they die, will live, and everyone who lives and believes in me will never die" (John 11:25–26). We stand before a great mystery: we do not die into death; we die into God.

Also, there are hints of this mystery of life beyond life. There are numerous stories of the wondrous in and around death in the tradition of the church, as well as the near- and around-death experiences we hear about through the media. Great Christian figures, such as Pope St. Gregory the Great, kept numerous accounts of death-related visions. Scholar Carol Zaleski explored these accounts in depth in *Other World Journeys: Accounts of Near-Death Experience in Medieval and Modern Times.* Many of these older accounts parallel the modern accounts. A person dies, leaves the body, meets a heavenly light, and then returns to tell the story.

Such stories by no means prove life beyond death, but they do provide strong hints of comfort in the face of death. One form of those types of encounters are visions and other such experiences that dying people sometimes have before they die, for instance, visions of loved ones or angels beckoning. One man told me of his dying father outstretching his hands, having a look of sheer gladness on his face and saying, "The angels are so beautiful."

Other experiences called "parting visions" are visions people have of sensing the presence of the loved one, or actually seeing the loved one, soon after their death. A friend of mine, Paul Oswald, was dying with AIDS. He was leaving behind a wife and two little children, and he had suffered acutely from his illness. I was with him at the moment he breathed his last. I didn't have a vision, but in an extraordinary way I sensed angels in the room gathered around him. Afterward, I asked the two other people in the room what they felt. Each immediately said "angels."

One instance of "around-death visions" touched my inmost

soul. The year was 1994; Robert Herrmann and I were asked to give the parish mission to the Cathedral of Christ the King in our neighboring archdiocese of Atlanta.

As I gave the first talk, I was suffering from sinusitis, exhaustion, and a low-grade fever. I did not feel like being there. When I finally finished, a woman in her early thirties came up to speak with me. I am always glad to speak with people after a talk. Inside, though, I prayed, "Dear Lord, don't let this be another family problem. Any other time, but not tonight."

We went to a side chapel for privacy and her story poured out of her. "A year ago, my nine-year-old son died of leukemia. When he was first diagnosed, his father, my husband, abandoned us; he could not bear the weight and responsibility of that diagnosis.

"The last two weeks of my son's life he suffered greatly and was in the hospital. Despite this, each morning he woke with a smile on his face and said, 'Mother, I like it when I go to sleep at night because I go to a place where Jesus, the children, and the angels are in the heavenly light. And I play with Jesus and the children and the angels in the heavenly light.'"

Then she related that one evening her son opened up a subject she had not had the courage to bring up with him—his impending death. He said to her, "I know I am going to die soon."

She couldn't say, "Oh no, you are in the hospital, where people get better; you will get better too," or, "A new medicine will save you." She couldn't say anything like that because it would not be true. Instead she said and did the only thing a mother could say or do when confronted with such words from a child. She enfolded him in an embrace. As she held him, she said over and over again, "I love you, I love you, I love you."

When she had finished her son said to her, "Don't be so sad, Mother, because one day you can be with me and Jesus and the children in the heavenly light." He continued, "Mother, I would like for you to feel what it is like to be in the heavenly light. May I place my hand on your forehead and give you a blessing from heaven?"

His mother nodded yes and he placed his hands on her in blessing. She told me she felt a stream of brightness, a light warmth, and consolation pass through her from the top of her head to the tips of her toes.

Two days later, her son died.

Several weeks after this as she was sleeping one morning, just before the alarm went off to get her up for work, she dreamed a vivid clear dream of her son appearing to her surrounded by heavenly light. He smiled at her and said, "Mother, I love you too."

The woman told me that she recounted this story to me because she knew I was struggling for inspiration and she thought the story would strengthen me. She asked if she could pass on her son's blessing to me. She asked if she could put her hands on my head in blessing. I said yes, and when she did, I felt a powerful force of brightness, light, comfort, and consolation pass through me from the top of my head to the bottom tip of my toes. I felt refreshed.

⇒ TIME FOR CALMING PRAYER ⇐

A Prayer ❃ *Lord, sometimes I tremble at the thought of my own death. I fear the suffering of it; I fear the unknown. It comforts me to know that you trembled too, at the prospect of your death. You abandoned yourself to the arms of the Father as you sweated blood. There are times I shrink from the prospect of death. You, my big brother, have already taken that journey, and I can abandon myself into your arms as you abandoned yourself into the arms of the Father.*

You are compassion incarnate; your touch can take away fear. Touch me now, Blessed Lord, and take away my fear. Catch my tears. You died so that dread may be forever cast down and replaced with hope.

You walked through death's dark doors into God's everlasting arms. Help me to rest my heart in those same arms, now and forever.

Scripture Reflection ❃

What I am saying, brothers and sisters, is this: flesh and blood cannot inherit the kingdom of God, nor does the perishable inherit the imperishable. Listen, I will tell you a mystery! We will not all die, but we will all be changed, in a moment, in the twinkling of an eye, at the last trumpet. For the trumpet will sound, and the dead will be raised imperishable, and we will be changed. For this perishable body must put on imperishability, and this mortal body must put on immortality. When this perishable body puts on

imperishability, and this mortal body puts on immortality,
then the saying that is written will be fulfilled:

> "Death has been swallowed up in victory.
> Where, O death, is your victory?
> Where, O death, is your sting?"

The sting of death is sin, and the power of sin is the law. But
thanks be to God, who gives us the victory through our Lord
Jesus Christ.   1 CORINTHIANS 15:50–57

Guided Meditation ❈ Let yourself grow quiet. Slowly
repeat the name of Jesus with every breath. As you breathe,
you notice your worries and tensions leaving. Rest a moment
in the quiet. Jesus comes and sits beside you. You feel so at
ease with Jesus near you: safe, so very safe.

While he is so close tell him of your fears and worries.
The busyness and preoccupations of the day drain from you.
You notice a glow of light that surrounds Jesus, the Light
of Resurrection. That light now encompasses you too. You
breathe in the quieting glory; your whole body absorbs the
light.

You are now ready to talk to Jesus about your fear of death.
Perhaps memories of the first time you were frightened by
death as a child, or memories of the time you lost a loved one.
Jesus now stands and you now see his wounds: his hands,
his feet, and his side. His wounds are afire with the flaming
love of the Resurrection, the already arrived New Creation.
You sense beams of light from those wounds that flow like

a searchlight into your heart, soothing and comforting you. They let you know that though you may not understand death and fear, you know Jesus has been through that dark door into glory. Though you may not understand, you have the brother who has walked ahead with you. Rest in that peace a while.

CHAPTER ELEVEN

How Inner Peace Leads to Compassion

Jake was a close friend of mine at my Presbyterian college, Belhaven. Like me, he was studying to become a Presbyterian minister. He was the son of missionaries to South America and was very devout. He headed a ministry for evangelical students that met for student-led devotions once a week. He possessed an uncanny spiritual sensitivity. There was usually a large crowd, and he was a superb presider. The teachings he gave those nights came from his heart and went straight to the heart of his audience. His eyes would moisten when we sang an especially moving hymn. In addition, he was one of the two or three most popular students on campus, belonging to a prestigious college social club. Then something changed that would cause him to lose all this.

The change began when, almost suddenly, the sweet devotional feelings that had sustained Jake went away; he no longer teared up as he led devotionals. The faith that had so sustained him no longer was his fortress. Something big was missing and he was not sure what it was.

It was the era of Mississippi Burning, when the Klan was powerful. It was the last few years of segregation. Almost all the churches in Jackson, Mississippi, were segregated. Many had members of the board of elders, called an elder guard, stand in the doorways Sunday mornings to turn away any African Americans who might want to worship with the congregation.

One Sunday morning, Jake saw the elders turn away a lovely African American couple with a boy and girl under ten. This struck Jake to the core; this was certainly not right or just. If they could not worship in the church, neither would he. He considered that moment a break with his past.

I had made the decision weeks before that I would not worship in a segregated church. I drove a car full of Belhaven students to the one African American Presbyterian church, Faith Presbyterian, to worship in an integrated congregation. Jake asked me if he could join us on Sundays. He involved himself in ecumenical, integrated social ministries. He resigned as leader of devotionals and became involved in the dangerous work of voter registration. When Dr. King led a March through Mississippi, he joined in. He lost his easy faith, yet found a different and deeper faith. His body and soul welled up a powerful compassion. He found a deep-down peace he had never known before.[25]

We cannot have peace within unless we feel and express compassion. We cannot express compassion if we do not open our hearts wide to God's peace. Christ said, "My peace I leave with you, my peace I give to you" (John 14:27). This is a cruciform peace shaped by his life of self-giving and his death on the cross.

During the World War II bombing of London, it was found that people who suffered from nervous disorders found unexpected health by forgetting their own troubles and ministering to the terrible needs of victims of the air raids. Often the reason many of us have no get-up-and-go, no liveliness, no joy, is that we are living only for ourselves.[26]

Dr. Karl Menninger, the famous psychiatrist and founder of the famed Menninger Clinic, was speaking to a group on mental health one day when a member of the audience asked this question: "What would you advise a person to do if that person felt a nervous breakdown coming on?" Everyone thought he would say to consult a mental health professional. To their amazement he answered, "Lock up your house, go across the railroad tracks, find someone who is in need, and do something to help that person."[27]

The English word *compassion* literally means "to suffer with." I clearly remember the day in advanced New Testament Greek class in college when Professor Walter Elwell explained the meaning of the Greek word that is translated "compassion" or "sympathy": *splagchna* or the verb form *splagchnizomai*. It literally means bowels, inward parts. It means to have so much compassion that it is felt in the inward parts. The gospels use this word of Jesus in instances when he encounters the sick, the hungry, the demon-possessed, the grieving, and the marginalized. Jesus feels compassion with his entire self, and the compassion does not stop there. Through compassion, he heals, reaches out, feeds a multitude, and most of all comforts his struggling followers with a tenderness that could only come from God.

He calls us all to have that same compassion, especially toward the most wounded, the most neglected, and the most desperate. We will never be truly at home with ourselves or at home with God until we, on a "gut" level, allow the pain of others and the pain of creation to touch us. Compassion allows us to get inside other people's skin and feel what they are feeling. Compassion is that state of mind that produces a thorough kindness and empathy that can ease the suffering of another. Compassion does not seek anything in return and does not further discord and anxiety. In short, it is a selfless loving kindness that leads to action to alleviate the suffering of others.

Deeply looking at others in our prayer transforms prejudice and discrimination into a loving kindness that pours out from our heart. If in our devotion we do not become aware that children are dying of hunger, that many of the elderly are hopelessly alone, that life is not respected and we have throwaway people, we are not praying; we are escaping. Jesus said, "Father, forgive them for they don't know what they are doing" (Lk 23:34). Those striking words tell us how to look out at those whom we think cause our suffering. The old saying "walk a mile in their shoes" applies here. In your prayer, think, "What is their life like? What suffering have they gone through? What oppresses them now?" When you do this, you look deeply into their soul and find a fellow sufferer.

Jesus calls us to compassion even for our enemies when he says, "Love your enemies, bless them that curse you" (Mt 5:44). When we can love our enemy, that person is no longer an enemy. When we look deeply into another during our prayer, we practice an effective way to change an enemy to an object of compassion. Then the person whom we considered an enemy now becomes our brother or our sister.

Whenever we bathe in the compassion of God and allow it to permeate us, it is far more likely we will lend a tender hand of help and compassion to our brother or sister. A frequent statement in the gospels was that Christ was moved with compassion. For instance, in Matthew 9:36, "When he saw the crowds, he had compassion for them, because they were harassed and helpless, like sheep without a shepherd."

The gospels are filled with scenes of Christ's compassion. One scene that John places at the beginning of his ministry (John 4:4–26) is Jesus' visit to Samaria. He breaks people's conception of how a holy person should act and repudiates the exclusiveness of the religious elite of his day that shunned Samaritans, branding them untouchable.

Even more important, in talking with the woman at the well, Jesus rejected the way religious society of his time treated "sinners." He knew her life was tainted. He knew that the world of his day had no problem with the act of degrading a woman, doubling the weight of sin upon her. While her partner was considered hardly guilty, her sin was deemed beyond forgiveness. Jesus neither scorned nor rebuked but made himself her friend and companion. The divine in him had fellowship with that which was human in her. His soul went out to her not as a hot blaze to burn up, but as a purifying flame. This text in John highlights two aspects of Christ's love: empathy with humankind and tender compassion for those who have stumbled.

The same Christ declared in Matthew that "Truly I tell you, the tax collectors and the prostitutes are going into the kingdom of God ahead of you" (Mt 21:31). He made it clear that sin does not remove the sinner from the tenderness of divine compassion.

When Christ showed compassion to the leper, he touched him (Mk 1:40–45). A word would have sufficed to heal him, but Jesus chose to touch. Lepers in Jesus' day were among the most outcast. They were forced to shout "unclean, unclean" whenever other humans approached. There was no need for Jesus to touch him. A word from him would heal the leper, but speech, even eloquent speech, would not express the tenderness and yearning sympathy of the Savior's heart. As the Scripture says, "moved with compassion, Jesus stretched out his hand and touched him, and said to him, 'I am willing; be cleansed.'"

Christ's tears of compassion come from his humanity, but in them we also confront a gentle sympathy, a loving kindness found in the very depths of God. Those tears are tokens of an endless ocean of compassion become human.

Jesus also tells the story of a Jew who was mugged, beaten near to the point of death, and abandoned along the road. A Samaritan came by, a man of a race the people of his time despised and considered no more than trash, administered first aid, took him to an inn to recover, and said he would return to check on him later (Lk 10:25–37). This biblical compassion is a compassion only the Holy Spirit can generate.

Compassion is one of humanity's loveliest abilities. It is a vital tenderness that combines an awareness of the suffering of others with a desire to alleviate it. Compassion brings dignity and grace to everyone who expresses it. It is central to Christianity.

God built us so that we can weep with compassion, even when it is an enemy who is suffering. We can sense another's grief, terror, or pain; we can feel tears well up in us when we see tears of profound misery or distress in another.

1 John 4:18 says: "There is no fear in love, but perfect love casts out fear; for fear has to do with punishment, and whoever fears has not reached perfection in love." Emmet Fox states: "It makes no difference how deeply seated may be the trouble, how hopeless the outlook, how muddled the tangle, how great the mistake (or misunderstanding); a sufficient realization of love (and compassion) will dissolve it all."[28]

We do not have to look hard to find suffering: the loneliness of a widow or widower now left alone, the hot anger and cold silences of a couple no longer able to communicate, the isolation and terror of a child who is being abused, and the violence of poverty on our most vulnerable people.

Compassion means we feel the pain of others and act to alleviate it. Only as we open up our hearts for God to calm our own inner storms can we calm the storms in others.

The apostle Paul, in beginning and closing his letters, often said, "I think of you whenever I pray to God." He could also say, "You are to me the aroma of Christ."

We encounter God in prayer, and we can encounter people in prayer. When we pray, we should not run from the people who make up the fabric of daily living but take them into our prayer. They are grist for the mill. Prayer thrives on the horizontal dimension.

People who suffer or who are victims of injustice are fuel for meditation. Try to get into their skin to feel what their life is like. Let yourself be moved by their suffering. Feel, if you can, what they feel. Let the love and compassion of Christ flow in you and through you into them. Think of concrete actions you can engage in to help them.

⇒ TIME FOR CALMING PRAYER ⇐

A Prayer ❈ *Dear Lord, you are an endless reservoir of compassion. In Jesus, you touched and you healed. You know the things we face daily, things like loneliness, fear, and anxiety. You felt these sorrows too. Therefore, you can soothe us and shed tears for us, and as you did with the Beloved Disciple, you take us to your bosom. Your compassion is the salve for the wounds on our heart, the only medicine that can truly bring peace. Just as Jesus healed people and physically touched them, he now heals and physically touches us in the Eucharist.*

Make our hearts tender; help us to weep with all who weep. Help us to embrace the neglected ones, the despised ones of our world. Send your Spirit that we may do more than feel their pain. Challenge us to give a cup of water, to do the deeds of compassion. Lead us to be bringers of peace as you are a bringer of peace.

Scripture Reflection ❋
Then Jesus went about all the cities and villages, teaching
in their synagogues, and proclaiming the good news of the
kingdom, and curing every disease and every sickness. When
he saw the crowds, he had compassion for them, because they
were harassed and helpless, like sheep without a shepherd.
MATTHEW 9:35–36

As God's chosen ones, holy and beloved, clothe yourselves
with compassion, kindness, humility, meekness, and patience.
Bear with one another and, if anyone has a complaint against
another, forgive each other; just as the Lord has forgiven you,
so you also must forgive. Above all, clothe yourselves with
love, which binds everything together in perfect harmony.
And let the peace of Christ rule in your hearts, to which
indeed you were called in the one body. And be thankful.
COLOSSIANS 3:12–15

Guided Prayer Experience ❋ In your imagination, you
are seated on a hill overlooking Jerusalem. Jesus takes your
hand, and you feel his compassion flow through your hand
into your body, soothing you, calming you, filling you with a
peace that is everlasting. Your worry, your anxiety, and your
fear quietly fade away in his presence.

Jesus looks down upon Jerusalem below, and you look too.
Jesus whispers in your ear, "They are like sheep without a
shepherd." In a wondrous way, your eyes look where his look:
at lepers covered with sores, women and children beaten and
abused, at men and women in fine rich clothes, so caught up

in power and status that they forget they need God and one another. Jesus begins to weep and spontaneously you do too.

Now in a way that only God can understand, you see other scenes appear before you, scenes from today's world. First you see people in your life today who are hurting. You and Jesus send out a heart-mending love on them. You can see their faces change from glum to peaceful. Jesus stands and spreads his arms wide to send out life-changing peace. You stand up too, to raise your arms to bless them. Then others join you, key people in your life who have loved you: your mother or mother figures, your father or father figures, your siblings, and those friends who are like siblings. Their presence strengthens your ability to bless and send out compassion and peace.

Then Jesus speaks to you and says, "Do more than feel compassion, allow your compassion to turn into deeds of mercy."

Notes

[1] Walter Brueggemann, *Living Toward a Vision: Biblical Reflections on Shalom* (Cleveland: The Pilgrim Press, 1982), 16.

[2] Bryan Chapell, *In the Grip of Grace* (Ada, MI: Baker Publishing, 1992), 136.

[3] Alexander MacLaren, *Sermons Preached in Union Chapel, Manchester* (London: Hodder and Stoughton, 1872), 44.

[4] https://w2.vatican.va/content/john-paul-ii/en/speeches/1987/september/documents/hf_jp-ii_spe_19870914_amerindi-phoenix.html.

[5] Quoted in Evelyn Underhill, *Mysticism* (Stilwell, KS: Digireads.com Book, 2005), 132.

[6] J.B.F. Wright, *Precious Memories* (1925).

[7] Philip A.C. Clarke, "A Lesson from Five Maidens," *The Works, Dynamic Preaching* (www.sermons.com).

[8] Walter Brueggemann, *From Whom No Secrets are Hid: Introducing the Psalms* (Louisville: Westminster John Knox Press, 2014), 154.

[9] Paul Guyer, "Kant, Immanuel (1724-1804)," *Routledge Encyclopedia of Philosophy*, https://www.rep.routledge.com/articles/kant-immanuel-1724-1804.

[10] *De Natura et Gratia*, cap. 43, CSEL 50, 270; PI 44, 271 Quoted in Bernard Häring, *Shalom: Peace—The Sacrament of Reconciliation* (New York: Farrar, Straus and Giroux, 1967), 138.

[11] Bernard Häring, *Shalom: Peace—The Sacrament of Reconciliation* (New York: Farrar, Straus and Giroux, 1967), 118.

[12] William Shakespeare, *The Merchant of Venice*, iv, sc.1,1.184.

[13] Leroy Huizenga, "Pope Francis: Conscience is Not Ego, Brings Freedom," *First Things*, June 20, 2013.

[14] Rev. Dr. Paul A. Lance, "Shepherd-Evangelists? An Unusual Choice!" December 28, 2014 (http://www.uccalpena.org/sermons/Dec%2028%20 Shepherd%20Evangelists.pdf), 4.

[15] Health Section, *The Advocate* (Stamford-Norwalk, CT), October 21, 2008.

[16] LaTonya Dunn, "Acceptance Requires Serenity, Wisdom," News, *The Albany Herald* (GA), August 28, 2012.

[17] Friedmann Schaub, M.D., *The Fear and Anxiety Solution* (Boulder: Sounds True Inc., 2012), 9.

[18] Max Lucado, *Fearless* (Nashville: Thomas Nelson, 2009), 10.

[19] Fulton Sheen, *Peace of Soul* (McGraw-Hill, 1949 excerpt: http://www.angelfire.com/ok3/apologia/anxiety.html).

[20] Madelin Adena Smith, "The Case of Conflict: How Do You React?" *Virginia Beach Metaphysical Spirituality Examiner* (Virginia Beach Examiner), May 11, 2010.

[21] Quoted by Karen Herzog, "Anger From a Spiritual Angle: Religious People Get Mad Too – And It's OK to Feel That Way," *The Bismarck Tribune* (ND), April 22, 1999.

[22] Matthew Heinrich, "Redemptive Suffering," In and Out of the Ditch, July 24, 2014 (http://inandoutoftheditch.blogspot.com/2014/07/redemptive-suffering.html).

[23] "William Sloane Coffin's Eulogy for Alex," *Now* (http://www.pbs.org/now/ printable/transcript_eulogy_print.html).

[24] Jerry Hayner, *God's Best to You* (Nashville: Broadman Press, 1982), comment 98485.

[25] This story is based on real events and real persons, but composites were used and some details changed to protect identity.

[26] http://webministries.info/sermons/ff5.pdf.

[27] Ibid.

[28] Quoted in http://www.quotes-positive.com/by/emmet-fox/.

PARISH RETREATS, MISSIONS, AND CONFERENCES

❊ ❊ ❊ ❊

The author of this book, Deacon Eddie Ensley, along with Deacon Robert Herrmann, offers parish missions, retreats, and conferences throughout the country. A parish mission by the two deacons draws the whole parish together. It recharges the congregation. Everyone takes time for the truly important things like wonder, mystery, healing, and prayer. People are reconciled. Faith is awakened. Vocations are discovered.

The deacons can also lead clergy retreats and conferences as well as religious education conferences.

To bring them to your parish or your event or to ask for an information packet about what their retreats and conferences can offer your area, you can contact them at **706-322-8840**, visit their website **www.parishmission.net**, or email Deacon Ensley at **pmissions@charter.net**.

> *"The Mission proved to be a tremendous help for our families... Our attendance was better than ever. The guided meditations throughout were vivid and uplifting. The parish mission was filled with solid content. The greatest compliment has been in the attendance."* **FATHER JOHN T. EUKER,**
> St. John the Baptist,
> Perryopolis, Pennsylvania